Donna Dewberry's
Quick & Easy Murals

Donna Dewberry

NORTH LIGHT BOOKS
CINCINNATI, OHIO
www.artistsnetwork.com

about the author

Donna Dewberry is a wife, mother of seven, grandmother and native Floridian and loves anything to do with painting, crafting and decorating. She has always been involved in decorating and redecorating her home and often someone else's, too. She loves making her home a place her family can be proud of. Even though usually on a very limited budget, she always used her painting ability and creativity to bring beauty and comfort to her home.

Donna is a teacher and author of four other North Light books, *Donna Dewberry's Complete Book of One-Stroke Painting*, *Decorative Murals with Donna Dewberry*, *Decorative Furniture with Donna Dewberry* and *Painting Garden Decor with Donna Dewberry*. Donna can be seen on the PBS and QVC television networks teaching her One-Stroke technique to hundreds of thousands of viewers.

Donna's One-Stroke painting workshop certification classes are taught all over the country. Also offered is a Two-Day Wall Seminar class for those who are interested in painting walls using the One-Stroke technique. And she also offers classes for those who want to become certified as a Home Decor Specialist or Wall and Furniture Specialist. Information on all of Donna's workshops can be found on her website, www.onestroke.com.

METRIC CONVERSION CHART

TO CONVERT	TO	MULTIPLY BY
Inches	Centimeters	2.54
Centimeters	Inches	0.4
Feet	Centimeters	30.5
Centimeters	Feet	0.03
Yards	Meters	0.9
Meters	Yards	1.1
Sq. Inches	Sq. Centimeters	6.45
Sq. Centimeters	Sq. Inches	0.16
Sq. Feet	Sq. Meters	0.09
Sq. Meters	Sq. Feet	10.8
Sq. Yards	Sq. Meters	0.8
Sq. Meters	Sq. Yards	1.2
Pounds	Kilograms	0.45
Kilograms	Pounds	2.2
Ounces	Grams	28.4
Grams	Ounces	0.04

Published by North Light Books, an imprint of F&W Publications, Inc., 4700 East Galbraith Road, Cincinnati, Ohio 45236. (800) 289-0963. First edition. Other fine North Light Books are available from your local bookstore or art supply store, or direct from the publisher.

07 06 05 04 03   5 4 3 2 1

Library of Congress Cataloging-in-Publication Data
Dewberry, Donna S.
    Donna Dewberry's quick & easy murals.
            p. cm.
    Includes index.
    ISBN 1-58180-302-8 (hardcover) -- ISBN 1-58180-300-1 (pbk.)
    1. Acrylic painting--Technique. 2. Mural painting and decoration. I. Title: Donna Dewberry's quick and easy murals. II. Title: Quick & easy murals. III. Title.
TT385 .D48423 2003
751.7'3--dc21

                                    2002033843

Editors: Gina Rath and Kathy Kipp
Production Coordinator: Kristen Heller
Designer: Joanna Detz
Layout Artist: Kathy Gardner
Photographers: Tim Grondin and Christine Polomsky

dedication

It is very difficult to single out one person for dedication of this book, but as my husband so eloquently puts it, it is my duty.

After some thought and recent reflections on and about my friends and loved ones, I have decided to whom I will dedicate this book. I am dedicating this book to four very important young ladies in my life—my daughters.

I would like to dedicate this book to Anna, age 16, Amanda, age 20, Kara, age 23 and Maria, who would have been 25. My daughters, not only do I love you, but I am proud of each of you and the young ladies you have become. I know we haven't always seen eye to eye, but you are and always will be treasures in my life.

I love each of you and am honored to be your mother. You are talented, each in your own way, and I truly admire this uniqueness. When counting the blessings in my life I am forever thankful for each one of you.

Thank you!

acknowledgments

The question has been asked of me many times, "How do you do all that you do?" Let me answer that question simply. I do not do it by myself. I am always surrounded by people who surprise me with their expert knowledge and abilities, which is what it takes to create a book of this calibre. I am ever thankful for their assistance and the great spirit with which they do their respective jobs. The list of people involved with the creation of this book is extensive. I was going to attempt to name them all but I'm afraid I will leave someone out. As I write this, I realize how blessed I am for each of you who has touched my life while making this book. Thank you.

table of contents

introduction

I think the very best compliment I can receive from my customers is: "You know, I feel as though I have known you forever." What that translates to in my business has been phenomenal, not so much monetarily as that my customers are comfortable and confident with my abilities and judgment. My experience as a mother, housewife, decorative painter, crafter and informal designer has given me certain skills that probably were learned only through those channels. I firmly believe that all of us are in possession of certain talents and that we can do anything we put our minds to.

I know that many of you think that you will be painting only in your own home, which may be the case. But others of you will find painting so enjoyable and the compliments so encouraging that you may soon find people asking you to paint for them. I know it seems scary painting for someone else, but go ahead and take the plunge. I did it— so can you!

I want to share something with you. My first wall painting job (other than for my family) was an experience I'll probably never forget. After the initial discussion with the customer over the phone, I was feeling pretty confident, but when I actually showed up at her house, my premature confidence quickly faded. I faced the day of reckoning. There was this blank wall and it seemed to grow larger by the minute. My hands began to tremble. I was terrified! What was I going to do? All that confidence was vanishing before my eyes. Here I was with the customer carrying on about how excited she was that I was actually going to paint a "work of art" on her wall. Talk about pressure!

I'm not sure just how I mustered up the courage to begin, but begin I did. You know what's amazing to me is that when I did begin to paint I felt much more at ease, and before I knew it the painting began to take shape. Now I'm not going to tell you that this was my best painting job ever, but I can assure you, it was my most memorable. Finally, after five hours I completed my painting and then the real payoff came when this customer stood back and commented that she was indeed happy, so happy that she became a little emotional.

Never had I experienced such satisfaction, not so much in my accomplishment but more in that someone else found worth in my painting. I must admit that I left a little piece of my heart on that wall that day and have done so on every job since. Discover for yourself, try it, share it, and before you know it you will have that same feeling that only wall painting can bring.

The designs in this book are quick and easy and can be adapted to your specific decorating needs. I want to encourage you to paint these designs without relying on patterns; therefore I have included patterns for only three of the twelve projects. However, if you really feel that you need a pattern for a particular project, you can always trace the full-page picture at the beginning of the project and make your own pattern. Feel free to change the colors to match your decor. I want you to be the designer in this book. Take my ideas and use them as a starting point for creating one-of-a-kind murals for your home. If you are ready to begin painting in other people's homes, take this book with you and use it as a visual reference while discussing ideas with your customer.

For those of you who feel you may want to begin your own painting business, I have included a chapter at the end of this book, "Starting Your Own Muraling Business."

Painting is a wonderful way to make some extra money while sharing your talent with others. Good luck!

supplies & basic painting techniques

PAINTS AND MEDIUMS

Plaid FolkArt Paints

Plaid FolkArt Acrylic Colors are high quality bottled acrylic paints. Their rich and creamy formulation and long open time make them perfect for decorative painting. They are offered in a wide range of wonderful premixed colors and in gleaming metallic shades.

Plaid FolkArt Artists' Pigments

Artists' Pigments are pure colors that are perfect for mixing your own shades. Their intense colors and creamy consistency are wonderful for blending, shading and highlighting. Because they're acrylic paints, they're easy to clean up.

Plaid FolkArt Floating Medium

Floating medium allows the paint to stay wetter, thus aiding you with your brushstrokes. When painting the one-stroke techniques, please do not follow the instructions on the bottle. This will make your strokes very muddy.

Instead, load your brush as instructed on page 11, then dip the tip of the bristles straight down into the puddle of floating medium. Stroke two or three times on your palette, then you are ready to paint.

Wall Paint

I have found that most people wait about five years before repainting their walls, so if the walls have not recently been painted begin your project with a fresh coat of interior latex or acrylic paint.

I prefer to paint wall murals or borders over a satin or eggshell finish rather than a flat or high gloss finish. The satin and eggshell finishes allow for even and smooth strokes and also allow you to easily remove mistakes without rubbing the base paint off. When painting borders and murals I always carry a really wet white rag with me to immediately wash off anything that I am not happy with, and satin or eggshell finishes make this easy to do.

I don't recommend painting borders or murals over a flat or a high gloss paint. I have found that a flat finish absorbs the paint and therefore does not allow your brush to glide over it easily. Also, mistakes on a flat finish do not easily wipe off. High gloss surfaces are too smooth and don't allow the paint to properly adhere.

Painter's Tape

When painting, it's important to use only tape that is labeled as painter's tape. Painter's tape is less sticky and won't pull off paint from the wall. Do not use masking tape; it will pull off the paint and can leave a sticky residue.

Flat Brushes

Painting the one-stroke technique requires the use of flat brushes. The large flats and scruffy brush shown below are especially useful for painting wall murals and borders. I have also designed a complete set of One-Stroke brushes that have longer bristles and less thickness in the bodies of the brushes to allow for a much sharper chisel edge. A sharp chisel edge is essential to the success of the one-stroke technique, as most of the strokes begin and then end on the chisel edge.

These brushes are ready to use from the package. Simply dampen the bristles in water and dry with a paper towel before beginning to paint.

If you clean your brushes in a plastic water basin that has ridges in the bottom, you may rake these brushes across the ridges to clean the paint out; the bristles are not made from natural hair and therefore do not have as much of a tendency to break, but be gentle.

Scruffy Brushes

The scruffy brushes that I have created are ready to be used straight out of the package. All you have to do is "fluff the scruff" as we say. Remove the brush from the packaging and fluff the natural hair bristles by gently pulling them open. Then, twist the bristles in the palm of your hand until you have a nice oval shape. Now you are ready to pounce the scruffy into paint and begin. Do not use this brush with water.

When fluffed, the scruffy brush can be used for painting mosses, wisteria, lilacs, certain hair and fur and for faux painting and shading textures. To clean the scruffy brush, gently pounce the bristles into the brush basin. Do not rake them or you will break the natural hair bristles. See pages 20-21 for how to use the scruffy brush.

Liners

There are two sizes of liners. The no. 1 script liner (sometimes referred to as the mini) is usually used for small detail work where more control is needed. The no. 2 script liner is a bit longer and is used where less control is needed.

Liner brushes are used with paint of an "inky" consistency. To acquire this consistency, pour a small amount of paint onto your palette. Dip the liner brush into water, then touch the water to your palette next to the paint. Do this three or four times. Roll your liner brush where the water and paint meet to mix them until you have an inky consistency. Don't mix all of the paint with the water or your mixture will be too thick. Roll the brush out of the inky paint to prevent it from dripping. See page 22 for how to load the liner brush.

Clean these brushes as you do the flat brushes. Once again, be gentle, but clean thoroughly.

Large scruffy

1-inch (25 mm) flat

1 ½-inch (38 mm) flat

Small scruffy

no. 1 script liner

no. 2 script liner

no. 2 flat

no. 6 flat

no. 8 flat

no. 10 flat

no. 12 flat

¾-inch (19mm) flat

Scruffy

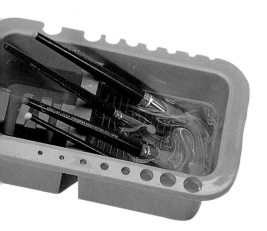

9

Working Without Patterns

You will notice that I have not included patterns for most of the projects in this book. I want to encourage you to learn to paint without relying on patterns. You will be surprised how easy it is and how creative you will become by painting freehand.

If you feel you must have a pattern for one of these projects, you can lay tracing paper over the large photo shown before each project and trace what you want to use. Then enlarge the pattern to whatever size is appropriate for your needs.

Transferring Patterns

To transfer a pattern to a wall, first enlarge the pattern to the size needed. You will probably want to transfer the design in stages, painting the background and letting it dry and then transferring more of the design. It is not necessary to transfer every detail; it takes away from the expressive look you are trying to attain. Since I encourage freehand painting, when I use a pattern or stencil, I normally use it only for the outline.

Lightly tape the pattern to the wall to keep it from sliding. (You may first want to trace the pattern onto tracing paper to protect the pattern for future use.) Use dark transfer paper for light walls and

light paper for dark. Place the transfer paper in between the pattern and wall (facing the wall) and trace over the pattern with a pencil or stylus.

When combining stencils with a pattern, use the pattern for placement of the stencil (just lightly indicate the stencil location) and then use the stencil for painting.

Stencils

There are numerous stencils available on the market. I prefer Plaid stencils and the two I use the most are the Picket Fence (shown in project 8) and the Bricks (project 9). The Urn stencil (project 9) and the Column stencil (project 7) used in this book are made of hard rubber and are reusable many times more than are Mylar stencils.

When using the picket fence stencil, look at the size of your room and decide where the fence will be placed and how tall you want it to be. To lengthen pickets, measure with a yard stick and level and tape off or draw a line. Use a white art eraser to erase any pencil lines that don't get covered with paint.

Palette

The FolkArt One-Stroke Paint Palette that I use is a durable and handy palette that allows you to keep paint and tools at your fingertips. The palette has numerous paint wells, holes for brushes and a base for paper towels. The palette is designed for left- or right-handed usage and holds a 9-inch (23cm) disposable foam plate.

What I especially like about the palette is the comfort. There is no need to grip the palette as it is designed to balance comfortably on your hand.

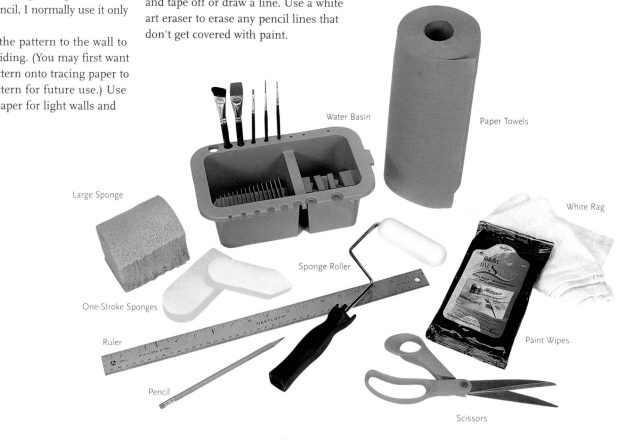

Stencils
Large Sponge
One-Stroke Sponges
Ruler
Pencil
Water Basin
Sponge Roller
Scissors
Paper Towels
White Rag
Paint Wipes

Double Loading the Flat Brush

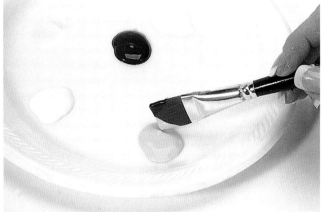

1 To double load, dip one corner of the flat brush into the first color. Make sure the brush is angled when you dip it into the paint.

2 Dip the opposite corner into the second color. This forms triangles on each corner of the brush.

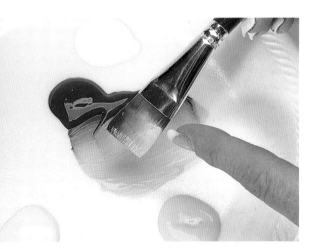

3 Brush back and forth on the palette, pushing down hard to work the paint into the brush. Don't spread the paint out too far on the palette (you will wipe the paint off of your brush); you want to work the paint into the bristles. Keep the area where you stroked on the palette no longer than about two inches (5cm) in length and the paint will stay in the bristles.

4 Repeat Steps 1, 2 and 3 a few times until you have worked the paint two-thirds the way up into the bristles of the brush. This is how your brush will look when properly loaded. Once fully loaded, dip each corner ever so lightly into its paint color one more time (don't stroke on your palette this time). Now you are ready to paint.

TIP ▶ When your brush is loaded correctly, your strokes should feel as though they glide. You do not have enough paint on your brush if the bristles split or if the brush grabs or skips as you're painting.

Floating Medium

If the bristles begin to feel dry, add floating medium. Dip a loaded brush straight into floating medium and work it into the bristles on your palette. Do not pick up floating medium more often than every third or fourth stroke.

Watch the Brush Handle

Watch the handle of your brush. Always keep it perpendicular to the surface. That way the brush bristles will do all the work.

Multiloading

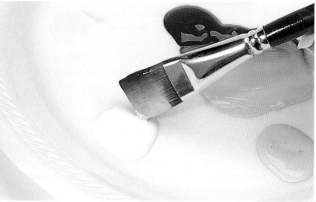

Double load a flat brush using two colors as shown on page 11. To multiload, ever so lightly dip the light corner (yellow as shown here) of the brush into a third color (white as shown). You can add even more colors if you want. Add darker colors to the dark corner of the brush and lighter colors to the light corner of the brush.

Painting with the Chisel Edge

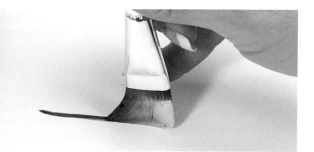

Properly load the brush, then, leading with the lightest color, touch, tilt back slightly lifting the yellow bristles, then pull.

TIP ▶ What do I mean by "Stay up on the chisel edge" or "Lift to the chisel"? You will see these instructions throughout the projects. It simply means your brush bristles will be touching the surface only along their very edge; you will not be applying so much pressure that the bristles bend completely and the flat side of the brush is against the surface.

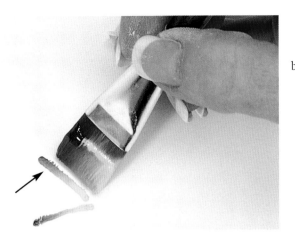

1 Double load the brush with two colors. Use the chisel edge of your brush to make a V. This is where you will begin each side of the leaf.

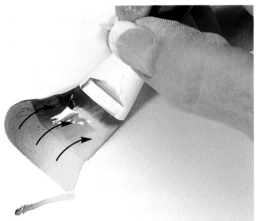

2 Begin with a starter stroke. Every time you load up your brush with paint and before you stroke the first half of the leaf, you need to do a starter stroke. A starter stroke is three strokes right on top of each other. Just touch, push down, then lift, three times in the same spot. The starter stroke spreads the bristles and blends the color. After the third starter stroke, begin the first half of the leaf.

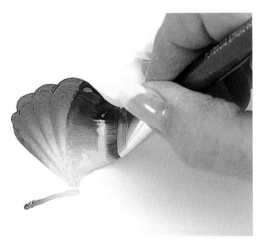

3 Go back to the line again and start wiggling the brush in and out, pivoting around the light edge to create a seashell shape. Keep your eye on the outside (green) edge of the leaf. This edge forms the shape of the leaf.

TIP ▶ If ever you don't like how your leaf looks, just go back and restroke the leaf right over the wet paint.

4 Once you see the seashell shape, lift and slide evenly up to the chisel edge of the brush to end the leaf stroke.

5 Repeat the steps for the other half of the leaf.

6 Pull a stem halfway into the leaf. With your brush on the chisel edge, lead with the light color and pull the stem halfway into the leaf.

TIP ▶ Keep your elbow off the table! This is also a good rule for painting leaves. If you prop your elbow on the table you will find it very difficult to create this leaf properly.

1 Multiload a 1-inch (25mm) flat with Thicket and Burnt Umber on one side and Sunflower on the other. Begin the leaf with a V, just as you did for the heart-shaped leaf. Wiggle out and slide back in halfway, then wiggle out again for the second section.

2 Again, slide back in halfway and wiggle out for the third section. Slide and lift up to the chisel edge of the brush.

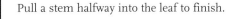

3 Repeat for the other half of the grape leaf.

4 Pull a stem halfway into the leaf to finish.

1 To add an interesting turned edge to your leaf (what I call "flipping a leaf"), begin painting the first side of a heart-shaped leaf as instructed in Steps 1 through 4 on pages 13 and 14.

2 Paint the second side of the leaf to the halfway point.

3 Then lift up to the chisel edge and flip the brush so that the green edge in now on the inside.

4   Pivot the brush and push down again. Note where the green edge of the leaf is now.

5   Lift up to the chisel edge and slide to the point.

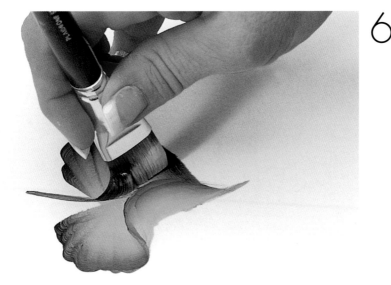

6   Pull a stem halfway into the leaf.

1 Shadow leaves are great for filling in backgrounds and adding depth to a painting. Load a flat brush with colors such as Burnt Umber and Thicket, then "clean out" the brush in a puddle of floating medium on the palette. Use this subtle transparent mixture to paint shadow leaves.

2 Rake most of this "dirty" floating medium off of the brush onto the edge of the palette.

3 Paint transparent one-stroke shadow leaves and stems with the mixture. Begin on the chisel edge of the brush, then push down on the bristles, turn and lift back up to the chisel edge to create the tip of the leaf.

You can use your fingers as a guide to help you with designing leaf direction. Hold your hand out and open up your fingers, noticing the direction your fingers point as you tilt your hand. This is similar to the direction that leaves grow from a vine. You'll achieve a more natural look to your vines and garlands if you'll check your leaf direction this way.

Floating a Shadow

1 Load most of a flat brush with floating medium, then side load the edge of the brush with a color.

2 Create a trompe l'oeil shadow effect by floating the color side of the brush along the outside edge of the leaf. The floating medium helps soften the shadow so it is not harsh or hard-edged. Floated shadows can be used on almost any object where you want to enhance the effect of depth and realism.

1 Before using a scruffy brush, use your thumbnail to fluff and separate the bristles.

2 Then press and twirl the bristles in the palm of your hand until you have a nice oval shape. Now your scruffy is fluffed and ready to use.

Double loading the Scruffy Brush

1 To double load the scruffy, pounce half of the bristles straight up and down into the first color. Stay at the edge of the puddle of paint, not in the center.

2 Pounce the other half of the brush into the edge of the second color. The scruffy is now loaded and ready to use.

Multiloading the Scruffy

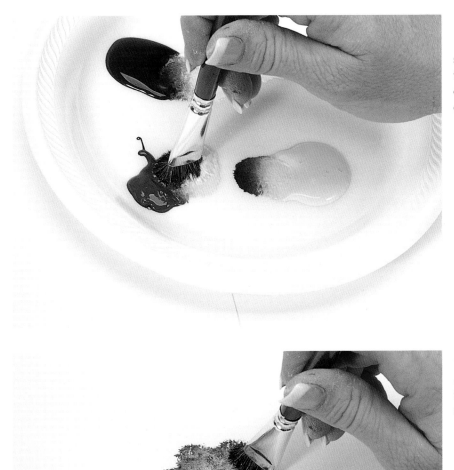

1 A scruffy can be multiloaded just like a flat brush. Follow the steps shown on pages 11 and 12. Remember to multiload light colors on the light side of the scruffy and darker colors on the dark side.

2 When using a scruffy brush you do not want to overblend by pouncing too much. You want to see the individual colors on the surface you are painting.

21

1 Dip a liner brush into water, then make a circular motion at the edge of the the paint puddle; repeat this a couple of times until you've achieved an inky consistency to the paint.

2 Roll the brush out of the inky puddle. Rolling the brush out helps you make sure the paint is inky and not watery or pasty. Rolling also prevents the paint from dripping.

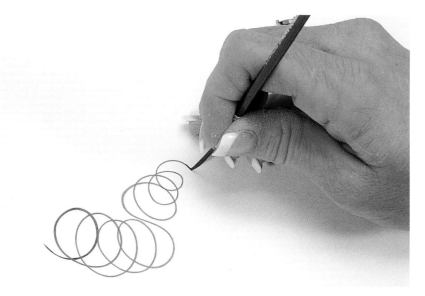

3 Keep the brush handle straight up and down while painting curlicues. Brace the brush handle against the second knuckle of your pointer finger, and use your little finger to guide you. Move your whole arm, not just your wrist.

1 When painting large areas like wall murals, you can use a sponge to cover the area quickly. Double load the sponge with two colors as shown. In this photo I'm using a One-Stroke Sponge Painter, which comes two to a set and has rounded or pointed ends.

2 Fill in the area using circular motions: this covers an area more quickly than just pouncing.

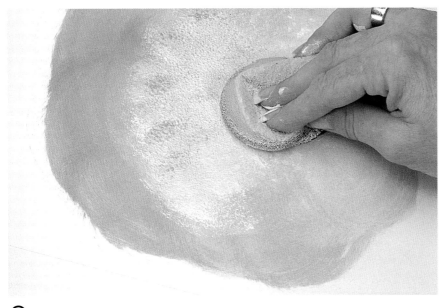

3 While the area you just filled in is still wet, load more paint onto your sponge and tap it in on top. This will soften the area by eliminating any lines.

six wall borders

HERE ARE SIX different border ideas that can add a special touch to any room in your home. They will look good either at ceiling height or at chair rail height, or topping off wooden or painted wainscoting.

You may copy these borders for your own home, or show them to your customers as idea-starters. I want you to be creative, so feel free to add as many or as few details as you like to any of the borders or murals in this book. Try taking some ideas from one border and some from another and combining them for a whole new look. It's fun and exciting—and if you don't like it, just paint over it!

Step-by-step instructions and photos for painting each of the six borders begin on page 28. The photos at right and on the following two pages show the completed, finished borders.

IVY BORDER
instructions begin
on page 28.

ROSEBUD BORDER
instructions begin
on page 35.

**FERNS & ROSES
BORDER**
instructions begin
on page 43.

HYDRANGEA BORDER
instructions begin on page 53.

DAISY BORDER
instructions begin on page 49.

FRUIT BORDER
instructions begin on page 57.

ivy border

THE IVY BORDER is my most versatile border. There are so many ways this border can be used once you have learned the simple painting technique shown on these pages.

Create your own design by adding different types of flowers, or try painting the vines as if they are growing out from the corner of a window or doorway. Change the colors to suit your decor if you want, but be sure to follow the instructions on loading the dark and light colors on your brush.

—— WHAT YOU'LL NEED ——

PAINT > Plaid FolkArt   (AP) = Plaid FolkArt Artists' Pigment

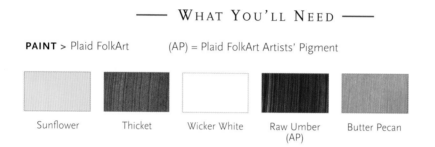

| Sunflower | Thicket | Wicker White | Raw Umber (AP) | Butter Pecan |

BRUSHES > no. 12 flat, 1-inch (25mm) flat, no. 2 script liner. **ADDITIONAL SUPPLIES** > floating medium, painter's tape. **PATTERN** > I encourage you to paint this border freehand, but if you need a pattern, trace the finished border shown on pages 24-25 and enlarge as needed. **SURFACE** > Interior wall painted with acrylic or latex paint in a satin or eggshell finish.

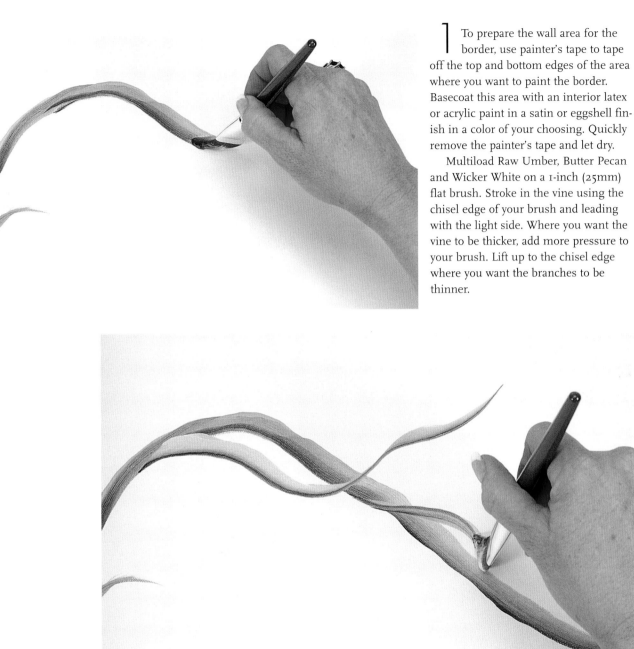

1 To prepare the wall area for the border, use painter's tape to tape off the top and bottom edges of the area where you want to paint the border. Basecoat this area with an interior latex or acrylic paint in a satin or eggshell finish in a color of your choosing. Quickly remove the painter's tape and let dry.

Multiload Raw Umber, Butter Pecan and Wicker White on a 1-inch (25mm) flat brush. Stroke in the vine using the chisel edge of your brush and leading with the light side. Where you want the vine to be thicker, add more pressure to your brush. Lift up to the chisel edge where you want the branches to be thinner.

2 Now add small branches off of the main branch alongside of and crossing over the main branch.

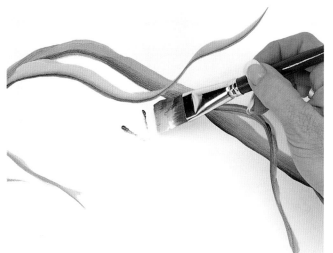

3 Still using the same brush you just used for the vine, pick up Thicket on the dark side and Wicker White on the light side of the bristles. To paint an angel-winged leaf, use the chisel edge of your brush to place a V-shaped starting point.

4 Begin with the three starter strokes, then stroke in the first half of the leaf, keeping the Thicket side of your brush facing up. Touch, wiggle and lift up to the point.

5 Stroke in the left wing-shaped side of the leaf.

6 Stroke in the right side of the heart shape.

7 Stroke in the left side of the heart shape.

8 Pull a stem into the leaf to finish. Stroke in a heart-shaped leaf next to it along the vine, using the same brush and colors, but picking up a little Sunflower on the White side of the brush.

9 Finish the heart-shaped leaf by pulling a stem into it from the main vine. To add variety, the next ivy leaf has one smooth edge. Follow the instructions on pages 30-31 for the first three sections of the angel-winged leaf. Then for the final section on this leaf, start on the chisel edge of the brush, lean the bristles out and smoothly come back up to the chisel edge as you slide to the tip. Do not turn the brush as you make this stroke.

10 Keep reloading the same brush with the same colors and fill in around the vine by adding some little one-stroke leaves. Be sure to start on the chisel edge of the brush, push the brush down and pivot the green (Thicket) side toward the tip. Lift back up to the chisel edge to finish the leaf. Immediately pull the stems from the vine into the leaves.

11 Add some filler vines if you wish. Remember to stay up on the chisel edge of your brush, and use floating medium if needed.

12 Using a no. 12 flat with floating medium and Raw Umber, add one-stroke shadow leaves here and there.

13 Continue filling in with shadow leaves, some on top and some below the main vine.

14 Use a no. 2 script liner and inky Raw Umber to add tiny root hairs to the vine.

15 Finish the ivy border by adding curlicues or tendrils using the same no. 2 script liner and paint color you just used for step 14.

The Completed Ivy Border

rosebud border

THIS LIGHT AND AIRY BORDER of blue hydrangeas, pink rose-buds and yellow butterflies can be used to bring sunshine into any room. Remember that any of the flower colors or the ribbon color may be changed to match your decor; you can even adjust the color of the leaves.

In this project you will learn step-by-step how to paint a rosebud. Once you see how quick and easy it is, you can add rosebuds to any of your decorative painting projects.

— WHAT YOU'LL NEED —

PAINT > Plaid FolkArt

| Thicket | Wicker White | Night Sky | Sterling Blue | Sunflower | Berry Wine |

School Bus
Yellow

BRUSHES > 1-inch (25mm) flat, no. 12 flat, no. 2 script liner. **ADDITIONAL SUPPLIES >** floating medium, painter's tape. **PATTERN >** I encourage you to paint this border freehand, but if you need a pattern, trace the finished border on pages 24-25 and enlarge as needed. **SURFACE >** Interior wall painted with latex or acrylic paint in a satin or eggshell finish.

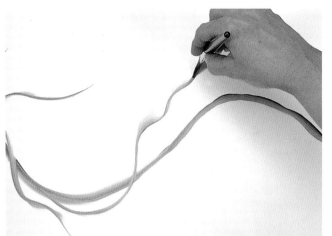

1 To prepare the wall area for the border, use painter's tape to tape off the top and bottom edges of the area where you want to paint the border. Basecoat this area with an interior latex or acrylic paint in a satin or eggshell finish in a color of your choosing. Quickly remove the painter's tape and let dry.

Double load a 1-inch (25mm) flat with Thicket and Wicker White and add a tiny bit of Sunflower. Staying up on the chisel edge of your brush and leading with the light side, paint in the main vine. Add some smaller vines coming off of and crossing over the main vine.

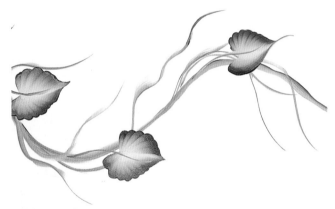

2 Using the same brush double-loaded with Thicket and Wicker White, add the large leaves. Since these are the first leaves you're adding to the vine, be sure to space them out so you can add smaller leaves and flowers later without having to crowd them in.

3 With the same brush and colors used in step 2, dip into some floating medium and add one-stroke leaves. Begin each leaf on the chisel edge, then push, turn and lift back up to the chisel for the tip of the leaf.

4 Double load Thicket and Wicker White on a no. 12 flat, dip into floating medium and add even smaller one-stroke leaves.

5 To start the center petal of the rosebud, double load Berry Wine and Wicker White on a 1-inch (25mm) flat. Begin on the chisel edge and keep the brush handle upright. Press down on the bristles and make an upside-down U-shaped stroke, keeping the Berry Wine side of the brush at the bottom.

6 To close up the center of the rosebud, add a second petal with a right-side-up U-stroke. Don't flip your brush over—keep the Berry Wine side of the brush at the bottom.

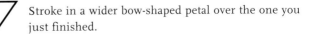

7 Stroke in a wider bow-shaped petal over the one you just finished.

8 Stroke another petal across the front of the bud by leaning the white edge of the brush outward and staying up on the chisel edge.

9 Pull in another petal stroke from the opposite side as shown. Lead with the Berry Wine side of the brush to keep the outer edge of the petal white.

10 Add some little one-stroke leaves at the base of the rosebud with Thicket and Wicker White.

11 Double load Sterling Blue and Wicker White on a no. 12 flat and paint a cluster of five-petal flowers. As you stroke these in, overlap them. If the green from the leaves is still a little wet underneath, you may find that you're picking up some of this color once in awhile; that's okay, it gives the hydrangeas a nice shaded look.

12 Continue adding and overlapping the five-petal flowers in a cluster.

13 Use the chisel edge of your brush to add a few petals that are seen from the side.

14 Add some trailing petals, if you want, using the same stroke; just don't push as hard.

15 Dip the tip end of the handle of your brush into Sunflower and dot in the flower centers.

16 Add ribbon and bows wherever there is adequate space. Double load Night Sky and Wicker White on a no. 12 brush. Begin on the chisel edge next to the vine and make large outward-curving strokes.

17 Wherever you want the ribbon to be wide, press down on the bristles and slide.

18 To make the ribbon look like it is turning, use the flat of the bristles and lean the brush to the right; go up to the chisel edge then lean to the left using the flat of the bristles; go back up to the chisel edge then lean to the right again on the flat of the bristles. If your ribbon starts to break up, you haven't loaded your brush with enough paint. See page 11 for proper brush-loading techniques.

19 Add the other end of the ribbon to the other side of the vine.

20 Tie the ribbon to the vine by painting the center of the bow with a simple C-shaped stroke.

21 Use inky Thicket on a no. 2 liner brush to add curlicues and tendrils.

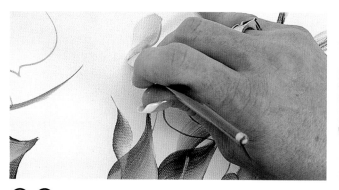

22 To paint the butterfly's back wing, double load School Bus Yellow and Wicker White on a no. 12 flat. Start on the chisel edge, push, turn and lift back up to the chisel edge to form the wing.

23 For the front wing, add more Wicker White to your brush so it can be seen more clearly, and paint the front wing at a slightly different angle.

24 Add the bottom two wings with two chisel-edge strokes. Use your no. 2 script liner with inky Thicket for the butterfly's body. Lay the bristles down and then pull as you lift up to the tip.

25 Add the antennae with just a touch and a pull.

The Completed Rosebud Border

ferns & roses border

ROSES ARE PERFECT for many rooms in the home. I especially like them in the bedroom and bath. You will be pleasantly surprised at how simple these large cabbage roses are to paint, and you've already seen how to paint rosebuds in the previous project.

There are two kinds of ferns in this border: a small, wispy fern and a fern with larger, longer leaves. I have varied the intensity of green throughout the border, as I have learned that keeping some ferns lighter really adds depth to the design and fills in the background so well that there's no need to use any filler flowers. Ferns and roses—simple elegance for your home.

—— WHAT YOU'LL NEED ——

PAINT > Plaid FolkArt

| Thicket | Wicker White | Berry Wine | Sunflower |

BRUSHES > ¾-inch (19mm) flat, 1-inch (25mm) flat, no. 6 flat, no. 12 flat. **ADDITIONAL SUPPLIES >** floating medium, painter's tape. **PATTERN >** I encourage you to paint this border freehand, but if you need a pattern, trace the finished border on pages 24-25 and enlarge as needed. **SURFACE >** interior wall painted with a latex or acrylic paint in a satin or eggshell finish.

1 To prepare the wall area for the border, use painter's tape to tape off the top and bottom edges of the area where you want to paint the border. Basecoat this area with an interior latex or acrylic paint in a satin or eggshell finish in a color of your choosing. Quickly remove the painter's tape and let dry.

Double load a ¾-inch flat with Thicket, Wicker White and floating medium and, leading with the white edge of the brush, paint in the fern stems.

2 Load a no. 12 flat with the same colors and paint in the branching stems for the small-leafed ferns.

3 Using the same brush and colors, stroke in little fern leaves. Start each leaf away from the stem. Touch down on the chisel edge, press down lightly as you pull in toward the stem, then lift back up to the chisel edge to finish.

4 To paint the shadow ferns in the background, double load a 1-inch (25mm) flat with Thicket and Wicker White, plus floating medium. Again, start away from the stem and pull in the leaves, curving them in to the stem. Keep these ferns a very light shade of green so they will remain in the background. If the color is too intense, use more floating medium in your brush. Restroke the center stem after you have pulled in the leaves.

5 Stroke in the darker foreground fern using the same brush with Thicket and Wicker White, but no floating medium.

6 Begin the cabbage rose by stroking in the outer apron. These are seashell shaped petals. Double load a 1-inch (25mm) flat with Wicker White and Berry Wine. Begin with a starter stroke to spread the bristles and blend the color. Keep the brush handle straight up and down with lots of pressure on the bristles. Stroke, push, wiggle, then lift. Each petal section is shaped like a fan, with the Berry Wine toward the center and the white along the edges.

7 Once you have completed the apron, stroke in the back petal of the center rosebud. Begin on the chisel edge and make an upside-down U-shaped stroke, ending on the chisel. Watch the light edge of the brush for the shape while you're painting.

8 Add the front petal of the rosebud. This time stroke in a U-shaped stroke from line to line. Remember, don't flip your brush. Keep the Berry Wine toward the center of the rose.

9 Add a second layer of petals around the rosebud. If need be, you can restroke the front of the rosebud at this time.

10 Add two more petals curving around from the side of the bud. Start on the line and lean the brush with the white facing out; then come across in front of the bud as you lift back up to the chisel edge.

11 Slide on the chisel edge and add the last little petal underneath the bud.

12 Now, with the same brush and paint colors, add the rosebuds to the border (see pages 37-38 for complete rosebud instructions). If you need help with the placement of the rosebuds, see the finished border on the next page.

13 Double load a ¾-inch (19mm) flat with Thicket and Wicker White and stroke in the calyx at the bottom of each rosebud. Touch the chisel edge of your brush and push and then lift, leading with the white. Add one on each side of the rosebud.

14 Add one short little calyx in the center of each rosebud.

15 For the rosebud stems, double load a ¾-inch flat with Thicket and Wicker White. Touch the bottom of the bud, lean on the chisel edge, and then pull and lift up to the chisel as you pull the stem away from the bud.

16 Multiload a ¾-inch (19mm) flat with Thicket, Wicker White and Sunflower and add large leaves on each side of the cabbage rose. Butt these up right next to the rose. Use a no. 6 flat with floating medium and Thicket and add little one-stroke leaves and stems (remember to pull the stems in right away), making little three-leaf clusters that are tucked in and around the roses.

The Completed Ferns & Roses Border

daisy border

THIS IS A FUN AND FRESH BORDER that will cheer up any room. You will be surprised how quickly this border can be painted; begin in the morning and you may be finished by lunch. Have your friends over for an afternoon treat and surprise them with your creativity.

You will be painting large white and yellow daisies on this border. Choose a complementary background color. I have chosen Purple Lilac, but you could use a soft green or any color that enhances your decor.

Note that if you paint this border on white walls, you should choose a color other than white for the daisies.

─── WHAT YOU'LL NEED ───

PAINT > Plaid FolkArt   (AP) = Plaid FolkArt Artists' Pigment

| Thicket | Wicker White | Purple Lilac | Grass Green | Licorice | Yellow Light (AP) |

Sunflower

BRUSHES > 1-inch (25mm) flat, no. 12 flat, no. 2 script liner, small scruffy. **ADDITIONAL SUPPLIES** > floating medium, painter's tape. **PATTERN** > I encourage you to paint this border freehand, but if you need a pattern, trace the finished border on pages 26-27 and enlarge as needed. **SURFACE** > Interior wall painted with latex or acrylic paint in a satin or eggshell finish.

1 To prepare the wall area for the border, use painter's tape to tape off the top and bottom edges of the area where you want to paint the border. Basecoat this area with an interior latex or acrylic paint in a satin or eggshell finish in a color of your choosing. Quickly remove the painter's tape and let dry.

Use Wicker White on a 1-inch (25 mm) flat to stroke in the large white daisies. Begin each petal on the chisel edge of the brush, push down very hard to form the widest part of the petal, then lift to bring the petal to a point. You want the petals to be transparent and the streaks to show through, so don't keep stroking over and over again. Overlap the petals as they radiate out from the center, then overlap the daisy blossoms somewhat.

2 Multiload a no. 12 flat with Wicker White, Yellow Light and Sunflower, and stroke in the smaller yellow daisies the same way you did the white ones. Don't blend the paint too much; it's good to have all the different shades showing in the petals.

3 When you paint a daisy seen from the side, make the back petals longer than the front petals and stroke them in first. Make sure the front petals are a little different tone (you can add a little more white) so they show up as front petals.

4 Double load Thicket and Grass Green on a no. 12 flat and add short little chisel-edged strokes at the bottom of the daisy to form a calyx. Pull the last stroke longer to create the stem.

5 Use Grass Green on the tip end of your brush handle to dot in the flower centers on the small daisies.

6 Load a small scruffy with Yellow Light, then dip one side of the bristles into Grass Green. Pounce in the centers of the large white daisies. Don't pounce too long or you'll overblend the colors.

7 Add the large leaves, using a 1-inch (25 mm) flat double loaded with Grass Green and Thicket. Exaggerate the rippled sides of the leaves by wiggling in and out randomly, then sliding the Thicket side of the brush to the tip of the leaf. Use the same brush and stroke in several long, one-stroke leaves.

8 Load a no. 2 script liner with inky Licorice to do the outlining. Just be very loose, don't try to outline anything exactly. Remember to use your little finger to steady the brush.

The Completed Daisy Border

hydrangea border

I LOVE HOW THE HYDRANGEA FLOWER accents a variety of decorating styles. It's so versatile—country, traditional, contemporary or oriental all work well with the hydrangea.

The color combinations of the blossoms can be changed to complement the colors of the room in which you are painting. If you are painting a room pink and peach, use these two colors for the blossoms. If the room has yellow and orange, those are your blossom colors. You get the idea—have fun!

——— WHAT YOU'LL NEED ———

PAINT > Plaid FolkArt   (AP) = Plaid FolkArt Artists' Pigment

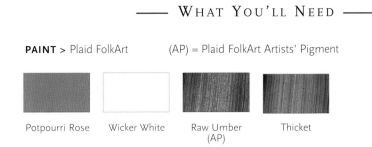

Potpourri Rose   Wicker White   Raw Umber   Thicket
                                     (AP)

BRUSHES > 1-inch (25mm) flat, no. 12 flat, no. 2 script liner. **ADDITIONAL SUPPLIES >** floating medium, painter's tape. **PATTERN >** I encourage you to paint this border freehand, but if you need a pattern, trace the finished border on pages 26-27 and enlarge as needed. **SURFACE >** Interior wall painted with latex or acrylic paint in a satin or eggshell finish.

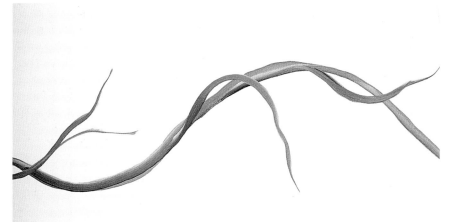

1 To prepare the wall area for the border, use painter's tape to tape off the top and bottom edges of the area where you want to paint the border. Basecoat this area with an interior latex or acrylic paint in a satin or eggshell finish in a color of your choosing. Quickly remove the painter's tape and let dry.

Use your 1-inch (25mm) flat double loaded with Raw Umber and Wicker White to paint in the main vine. Add additional smaller vines coming off of and crossing over the main vine.

2 These background shadow leaves will be behind the large leaves and hydrangea blossoms. Use your 1-inch (25mm) flat and a lot of floating medium with Thicket to paint in one-stroke and full-size leaves. Keep them very faint and subtle—these are shadow leaves.

3 Still using the 1-inch (25mm) flat, double load with Thicket and Wicker White and paint the large dark leaves. Since these leaves are very large, you will need to add floating medium to your brush.

4 You can achieve a wonderful variety of petal colors by alternating the colors you load onto your brush. Start with Potpourri Rose and Wicker White on a no. 12 flat and paint in a scattering of petals, keeping the Wicker White to the outer edges. Start each petal on the chisel edge, push up and over, then slide back to the chisel. Notice how you may occasionally pick up a touch of green from the leaves if they haven't completely dried, and that's okay. It adds a nice subtle color variation in the flowers.

5 Now with the same brush, pick up just a little Raw Umber on the Potpourri Rose side of the bristles and add more flowers over some of the previous ones. Reverse these two steps if you prefer to have more pink flowers showing.

6 Load Thicket and a little floating medium on a no. 12 flat and add clusters of one-stroke leaves to fill in along the vine.

7 Load a no. 2 script liner with inky Raw Umber and dab in the flower centers. Use just the tip of the brush, lightly painting several dabs in each center. Finish off with curlicues and tendrils.

The Completed Hydrangea Border

fruit border

I HAVE FOUND THIS BORDER to be a very popular design because of its versatility. Many fabrics have fruit and flower combinations, and you can easily adjust the type of fruit and the colors you use to match the fabric you have.

You can also use elements of this design to create branches or vines wandering around and out from windows, doors or corners. Wandering vines should appear to be continuous, even if interrupted by door or window openings or turning corners. I have found it helpful when planning the placement of vines around a doorway to stand back, look at the doorway and make sure the vine coming out of each side of the door frame has a flow to it, as if it were connected all the way through the door's opening.

—— WHAT YOU'LL NEED ——

PAINT > Plaid FolkArt   (AP) = Plaid FolkArt Artists' Pigment

Thicket	Wicker White	Berry Wine	Sunflower	Linen	Yellow Ochre (AP)

Dioxazine Purple (AP)	Raw Umber (AP)	Raw Sienna (AP)	Burnt Umber (AP)

BRUSHES > 1-inch (25mm) flat, no. 12 flat, no. 2 script liner. **ADDITIONAL SUPPLIES >** floating medium, painter's tape. **PATTERN >** I encourage you to paint this border freehand, but if you need a pattern, trace the finished border on pages 26-27 and enlarge as needed. **SURFACE >** Interior wall painted with latex or acrylic paint in a satin or eggshell finish.

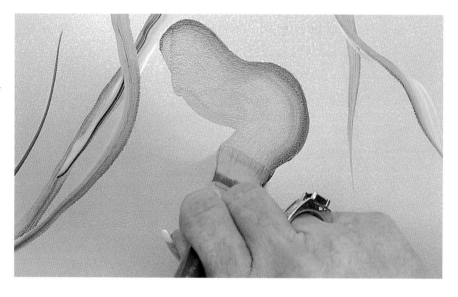

1 To prepare the wall area for the border, use painter's tape to tape off the top and bottom edges of the area where you want to paint the border. Basecoat this area with an interior latex or acrylic paint in a satin or eggshell finish in a color of your choosing (for this border I chose Linen). Quickly remove the painter's tape and let dry.

Begin by painting the vines using Raw Umber and Wicker White double loaded on a 1-inch (25mm) flat. Start on the chisel edge of the brush and lead with the white. Where you want the vine to be wider, add more pressure; where you want the vine to be narrower, lift up on the brush. Add smaller vines coming off of and crossing over the main vine.

2 To paint the pear, double load Yellow Ochre and Berry Wine (use more Yellow Ochre) plus floating medium onto a 1-inch (25mm) flat. Use the Berry Wine edge of the brush to draw in the shape of the right half of the pear.

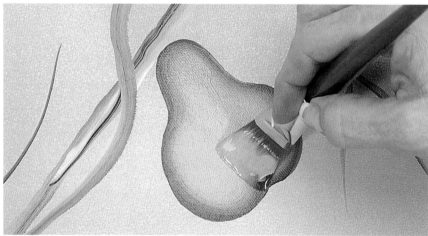

3 Stroke in the left half of the pear, still keeping Berry Wine to the outside edge.

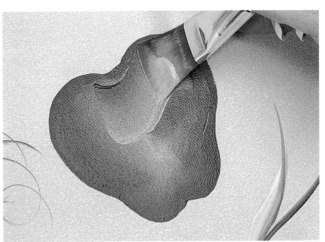

4 To paint the apple, use the same brush you used for the pear and double load Berry Wine and Yellow Ochre, loading more of the Berry Wine this time. Outline the apple as you did the pear, following the shape of the apple. Then fill in the center of the apple. Keep the Berry Wine side of the brush next to the outside edge.

5 Using the same colors and brush, paint the dimple at the top of the apple where the stem joins it. The Berry Wine edge of the brush creates the dimple. Stroke in a small U-shaped stroke across the upper part of the apple as shown. You can continue this stroke to the outside curve of the apple.

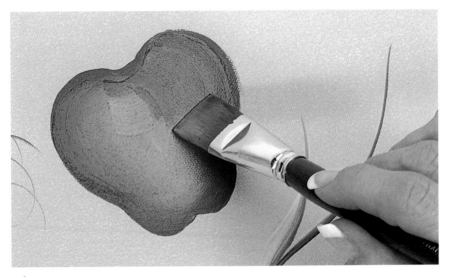

6 Wipe the brush off and dip the bristles into Berry Wine. Beginning at the dimple edge, touch and lay the bristles over as you lightly drag the bristles about halfway down the apple. Your strokes should follow the shape of the apple. Add a second stroke next to the first. This red accent adds roundness to the apple.

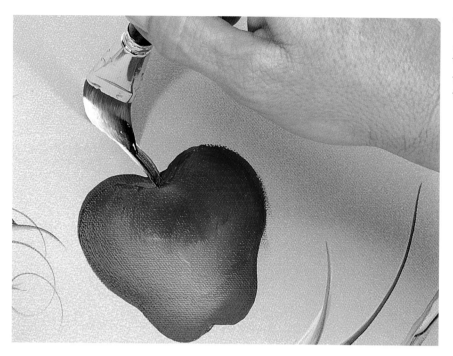

7 Double load a 1-inch (25mm) flat with Raw Umber and Wicker White. Leading with the Wicker White, use the chisel edge to pull a stem out from the apple.

8 Double load Thicket and Wicker White on a 1-inch (25mm) flat. Add some leaves at the top of each piece of fruit. Also add a large leaf for the grapes. The grape leaves are painted before you paint the grapes; any time you have a cluster of grapes, the leaves have to be painted first. Notice that the shape of the grape leaf is different from the leaves on the other fruit. Refer to the grape leaf painting instructions on page 15.

9 To paint grapes that have variations in color and shading, alternate the colors you pick up on your no. 12 flat. Start with Dioxazine Purple and Wicker White. After painting a few grapes, pick up some Berry Wine on the purple side of the brush and paint a few more. Keep the darker colors to the outside. Begin on the chisel edge, push and paint one side of the grape, then flip the brush and paint the other side. Restroke the grape if further blending is needed. Overlap some of the grapes to form the cluster.

10 Load a no. 2 script liner with inky Raw Umber, touch the tip of the liner into Wicker White and add the stems that connect the grapes to the vine.

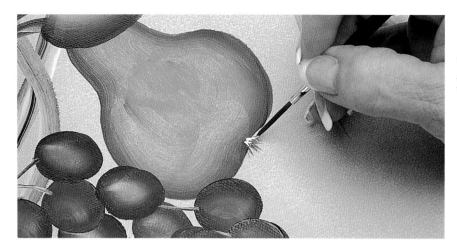

11 Pull tiny twigs from the bottoms of the pears using a no. 2 script liner and inky Raw Umber. Add highlights to the twigs with Wicker White.

12 To paint some shadow leaves in the background, use a 1-inch (25mm) flat with a lot of floating medium, Thicket, Wicker White and Sunflower (see page 18 for shadow leaf techniques).

13 Also add little one-stroke leaves using a no. 12 flat with Thicket and floating medium. You can stop at this point if you like the way your border looks, or you can add the brown leaves in the next step.

14 Use Raw Sienna, Burnt Umber and floating medium on a no. 12 flat to add the little brown one-stroke leaves. Pull the stems off the main vine and let the leaves overlap some of the fruit and larger leaves.

15 Finish off the border with curlicues if you like. Use a no. 2 script liner and inky Raw Umber.

The Completed Fruit Border

old world columns mural

THIS MURAL FEATURES the old-world look of faux marble columns, an archway with a lovely view, and a stone floor. Columns like these may be painted in a variety of locations in your home; I have painted a column in each corner of my dining room. Other places I've used them include both sides of a fireplace, a bed and a doorway, just to name a few. The stone floor in this design helps to give depth to the mural. The receding perspective of the tranquil landscape beyond the arch adds interest and invites you in.

—— WHAT YOU'LL NEED ——

PAINT > Plaid FolkArt   (AP) = Plaid FolkArt Artists' Pigment

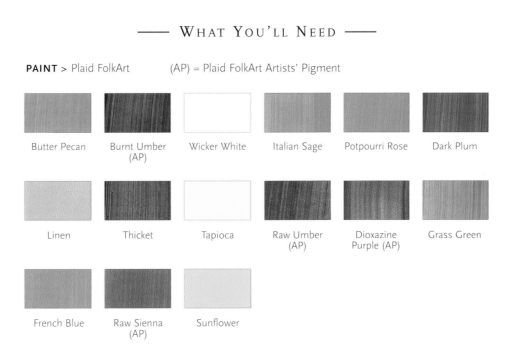

Butter Pecan	Burnt Umber (AP)	Wicker White	Italian Sage	Potpourri Rose	Dark Plum
Linen	Thicket	Tapioca	Raw Umber (AP)	Dioxazine Purple (AP)	Grass Green
French Blue	Raw Sienna (AP)	Sunflower			

BRUSHES > 1-inch (25mm) flat, no. 12 flat, no. 2 script liner, large scruffy. **ADDITIONAL SUPPLIES** > FolkArt One-Stroke Sponge Painters (or regular foam sponges cut to shape), floating medium, pencil, long level or yardstick (meterstick), Plaid's column stencil, plumb line, painter's tape.
SURFACE > Interior wall painted with latex or acrylic paint in a satin or eggshell finish.

This pattern may be hand-traced or photocopied for personal use only. Enlarge as needed for your wall space.

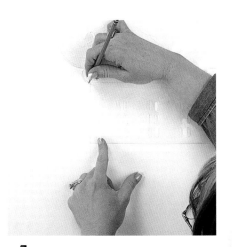

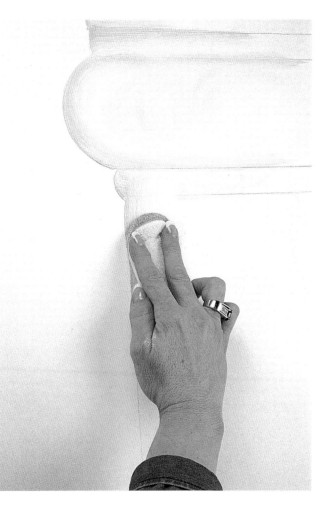

2 Use a long level or a level and a yardstick (meter) to draw the long sides of the column.

1 Make sure the wall area where you want to place this mural has been painted with a latex or acrylic interior paint in a satin or eggshell finish. Choose a color that harmonizes with the columns and stonework. Trace and transfer the pattern on the facing page to your wall, enlarging it as needed to fit your space. Use the column stencil to lightly pencil in the outside edge of the column. Use the same stencil for both the top and bottom of the column. See page 10 for helpful hints on transferring the pattern to the wall and using stencils.

3 Load the rounded end One-Stroke Sponge Painter (or a regular foam sponge cut to shape) with Tapioca and Linen. Pick up Tapioca first, then touch one edge of the sponge painter into Linen. Use the Linen edge of the sponge (the darker color) to outline the outside edge of the column. Then fill in the center using sponge circles (see page 23 for sponge painting techniques). Use the same sponge painter dipped into Butter Pecan to add shading to the curved top area.

4 Load the sponge painter with Tapioca and Linen and add random diagonal streaks to the column.

5 Add a little Potpourri Rose to the sponge painter and continue adding diagonal streaks down the column.

6 To help create the faux marble look, add veins here and there along the column. Use floating medium and Wicker White on a 1-inch (25mm) flat. Hold the brush lightly and stay up on the chisel edge.

7 Using the same brush with Raw Umber and floating medium, add a little bit of shading on one side of the veins.

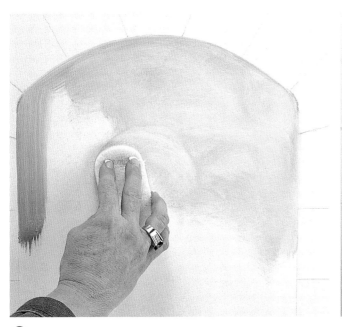

8 Begin the landscape seen through the stone archway by using a level to draw a straight line for the horizon that divides the sky and land. Apply painter's tape to the land side of the landscape. Load the sponge painter with French Blue, outline the sky area, then fill in the sky with circular motions of the sponge.

9 Add Wicker White to the sponge painter and pounce wispy clouds into the sky. Remove the tape at this time and allow the sky to completely dry before proceeding.

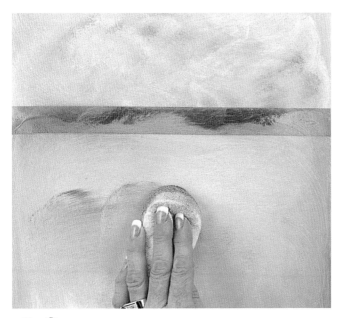

10 Apply tape over the very bottom edge of the sky area. Load the sponge painter with Sunflower, Wicker White and Grass Green, keeping Grass Green on the outside edge of the sponge painter. Outline the land area with Grass Green, then fill in using sponge circles.

11 This is how your landscape looks so far.

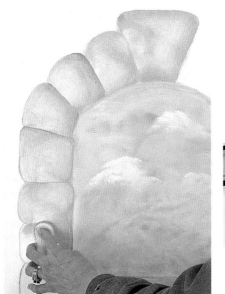

12 Load the sponge painter with Linen and Butter Pecan. Outline around each stone with the Butter Pecan edge of the sponge, then fill in with sponge circles. You will come back later and further define the stones.

13 Plan the placement of the stone floor. Using a level or yardstick, draw horizontal lines from column to column. To create the illusion of perspective in the stone floor, the horizontal lines must increase in width by $^{1}/_{2}$-inch (12mm) increments as they come forward. For instance, if the first row of stones below the base of the arch is 3 inches (8 cm) wide, the row below that would be $3^{1}/_{2}$ inches (9 cm) wide and the row below that 4 inches (10 cm) wide, etc. The bottom row should be the widest.

14 (Left) To establish a true vertical alignment of the stones, you will need a plumb line. You can make one yourself by using a push pin with a string attached and some kind of weight at the bottom of the string (an old key will do). Place the pin at the center of the highest point on the arch. When the string stops swinging, it will be perpendicular to the horizontal lines you have made. This is the center.

15 (Right) Make a vertical pencil mark indicating the divisions between the stones on every other row (top row, third row, etc.). Move the string 6 inches (15 cm) over to the right from the center pencil mark on the top row. Pull the string straight and mark the vertical divisions on the horizontal rows you have not yet marked (second row, fourth row, etc.). Repeat on the left side. Never move the pin from the center point, just move the string. The stones in each row will be longer as they come forward.

16 Place a piece of painter's tape along the bottom of the archway. Load Tapioca and Linen onto your sponge painter and use a back-and-forth stroke to fill in the stones. The Linen should be on the outer edge of each stone.

17 Use Linen, with floating medium if needed, to outline each stone.

18 Use floating medium and Raw Sienna, alternating with Raw Umber and Burnt Umber, to add more color to the stones.

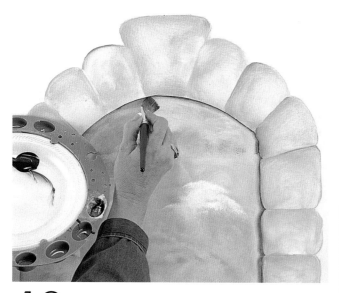

19 Use your 1-inch (25mm) flat brush with floating medium and Raw Umber to outline the inside edges of the stones in the doorway.

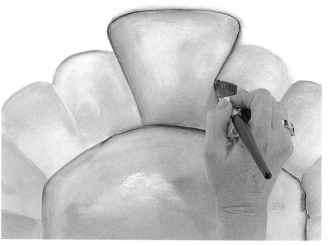

20 Still using the same brush and paint, shade the inside edge of the keystone, then shade the outside edge to separate the stones.

21 The left inside edge of the door-way has two lines of shading. This helps to create perspective. Continue using your 1-inch (25mm) flat with floating medium and Raw Umber to add the first line of shading.

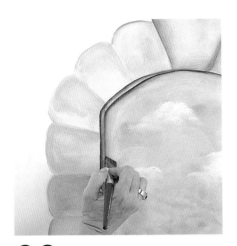

22 Add the second line of shading with the same brush.

23 Use the same brush and mixture to shade around the column edges.

24 This is how the mural looks now. If you like the mural at this point and want to keep it this way, that's fine. Stop when you are satisfied.

25 Using your 1-inch (25mm) flat with floating medium, Burnt Umber and Dark Plum, stroke back and forth to lay in the background for the trees.

26 Using the same brush and colors, define the edges of the forest pathway by wiggling your brush back and forth as you stroke. Lightly stroke back and forth in the lower area to give the look of uneven ground.

27 Add the tree trunks using the chisel edge of a 1-inch (25mm) flat with Burnt Umber and Wicker White, leading with the Wicker White. Keep the trees in the background shorter, then gradually make the trees taller as you come forward.

28 Use Italian Sage and Dark Plum with a little bit of Wicker White on your large scruffy to pounce in foliage on the trees. Also pounce in some short bushes inside of the tree line. This doesn't have to be perfect, you just want to create the illusion of a forest pathway.

29 Shade underneath the bushes with Raw Umber and floating medium on a 1-inch (25mm) flat.

30 Using the chisel edge of your 1-inch (25mm) flat with Raw Umber, Wicker White and floating medium, paint a vine on the right-hand column. It's important that you make the vine look as if it is growing up and around the column.

31 This is how the column looks with the vine completed. Do you see how the angle of each vine section is similar to the others? That helps give the illusion that the vine continues its upward growth around the back of the column.

32 Now paint a variety of leaves coming off the vines using your 1-inch (25mm) flat double-loaded with Thicket and Italian Sage. Connect the leaves to the vine with stems.

33 Use your large scruffy multiloaded with Dark Plum, Dioxazine Purple and Wicker White to pounce in some wisteria blossoms.

34 Detail some individual petals here and there on the wisteria with Dioxazine Purple and Wicker White on a no. 12 flat. Make little teardrop-shaped strokes. Begin on the chisel edge, push out using a downward C-shaped stroke, and end back up on the chisel edge.

35 Finish the wisteria vine and fill in any empty spaces with curlicues. Use a no. 2 script liner with inky Raw Umber.

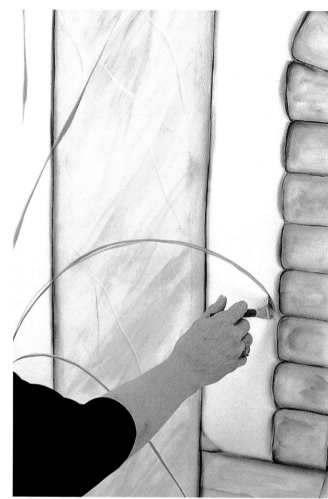

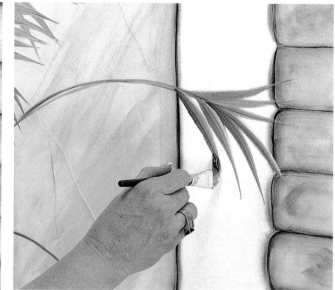

36 For the left-hand column, paint some large fern fronds that extend in front of the column. Place the stems first with Thicket and Wicker White on a 1-inch (25mm) flat.

37 With the same brush and colors, paint the fern leaves by stroking outward from the stem and then lifting to the chisel edge of the brush to form the point of the leaf.

38 Still using the same brush and paint, add the hanging leaves to the bottom fronds, crossing the front leaves over the back as shown.

39 This is the finished mural. I hope you use the elements that you like in
this design and make it yours!

welcome mural

THIS MURAL IS ONE OF MY MOST POPULAR designs and consists of a variety of elements. You can use as many or as few as you need. If you are painting a small space, use fewer elements—you don't want the area to appear crowded. For a large area you may need to repeat or add some elements.

When planning your design, begin with the largest element—the tree. I often like to place the tree in a corner or in an area where the bottom of the tree might be covered by a piece of furniture. Next decide how long and high you want the picket fence to be. Then you can fill in the mural with flowers, birds and butterflies.

Remember to adjust the colors to match your room decor. Most of all, have fun and be creative!

— WHAT YOU'LL NEED —

PAINT > Plaid FolkArt   (AP) = Plaid FolkArt Artists' Pigment

| Butter Pecan | Wicker White | Sunflower | French Blue | Yellow Light (AP) | Raw Umber (AP) |

| Pure Orange (AP) | Italian Sage | Engine Red | Night Sky | Licorice | Yellow Ochre (AP) |

| Dioxazine Purple (AP) | Thicket | Dark Plum | Berry Wine |

BRUSHES > no. 8 flat, no. 10 flat, no. 12 flat, 1-inch (25mm) flat, no. 2 script liner, large scruffy, small scruffy. **ADDITIONAL SUPPLIES** > FolkArt One-Stroke Sponge Painters (or regular foam sponges cut to shape), Plaid's picket fence stencil, floating medium, painter's tape, level or yardstick (meter), pencil. **SURFACE** > Interior wall painted with latex or acrylic paint in a satin or eggshell finish

This pattern may be hand-traced or photocopied for personal
use only. Enlarge as needed for your wall space.

1 Using the rounded-end One-Stroke Sponge Painter (or a regular foam sponge cut to shape), basecoat the sky with French Blue and Wicker White. Use a circular motion to fill in the sky, and add floating medium if needed for smooth application. (See sponge painting tips on page 23.) Notice that the sky area continues all the way to the ground behind the picket fence and flowers.

For demonstration purposes only, I have not painted some of the area where the tree is located. But it's best to paint all of the background (even where the tree will be).

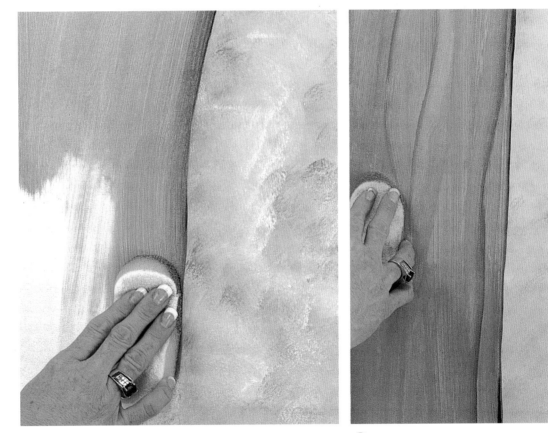

2 Once you decide where the tree will look best on your wall, trace and transfer the entire pattern to the wall over the basecoated sky. Still using your sponge painter, basecoat the tree trunk and branches using Raw Umber and Butter Pecan. Use plenty of paint and a straight up-and-down motion.

3 With Raw Umber on the outside edge of the sponge painter, lay in the texture on the tree trunk.

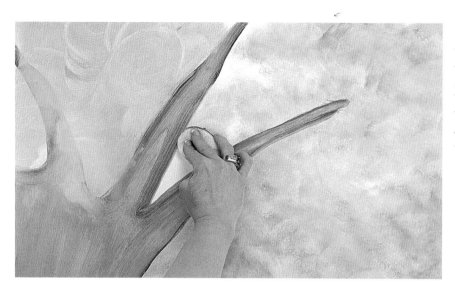

4 If you wish, paint just an indication of tree branches at the top of the trunk. This area will be covered by leaves, so don't spend too much time on the branches. With Italian Sage and Wicker White on your sponge painter, use a circular motion to fill in the background for the tree leaves.

5 With Wicker White on your sponge painter, add clouds to the upper sky area using a circular motion.

6 Multiload a 1-inch (25mm) flat brush with Thicket, Wicker White and Sunflower. Paint lots of leaves on the tree, but don't make them too dense and crowded. Use the same brush and colors to pull stems into the leaves, extending some stems out beyond the leaves for an airy look.

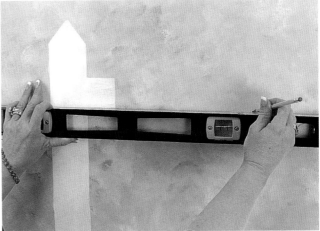

7 Using Wicker White, basecoat in the placement of the welcome sign and the birdhouse and post. Figure out where you want the picket fence to be, and tape the stencil to the wall with painter's tape (see page 10 for tips on using stencils). Use a level to make sure the stencil is straight and plumb. With Wicker White on your sponge painter, stroke in the first picket section.

8 Use a level to draw a straight line across the wall along the bottom of the horizontal crossbeams. This will make it easy for you to line up the rest of the pickets. Place the stencil and paint as many pickets as desired with Wicker White on your sponge.

TIP ▶ If you prefer, don't replace the stencil when you shade; just follow the shape of the picket with your sponge painter and add the shading. You have to be a little more careful, but it's quicker.

9 After the white has completely dried, shade the horizontal crossbeams. Lay the stencil back over the fence, then lay a piece of plastic (you can use the extra plastic piece you removed from the stencil) over the vertical boards to mask them. Paint the crossbeams with Butter Pecan side-loaded on your sponge painter.

10 Remove the piece of plastic from the vertical boards and shade them with Butter Pecan on your sponge painter. Use circular motions along the edges of the stencil; this covers the area faster than a brush does.

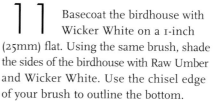

11 Basecoat the birdhouse with Wicker White on a 1-inch (25mm) flat. Using the same brush, shade the sides of the birdhouse with Raw Umber and Wicker White. Use the chisel edge of your brush to outline the bottom.

12 Using the chisel edge of your brush and the same colors, stroke in the thatched roof. Begin at the bottom and overlap the strokes as you go up.

13 Again with the same brush and colors, pull in the little point on top of the roof. Add the hole in the front of the birdhouse. Use the Raw Umber edge of your bristles to draw the outside edge of the circle.

14 Double load a no. 10 flat with Raw Umber and Wicker White and paint the perch and the ball finial.

15 Add the little white highlights in the hole and on the perch with a no. 2 script liner and Wicker White.

16 With a no. 2 script liner and inky Engine Red, add the ribbon and bow to the front of the birdhouse. The loops are painted with an outward motion, then pulled back in. Paint each loop as a separate stroke, picking up more paint for each stroke.

17 Shade around the welcome sign using a 1-inch (25mm) flat with Raw Umber and floating medium. Use the same brush to outline the rolled edges.

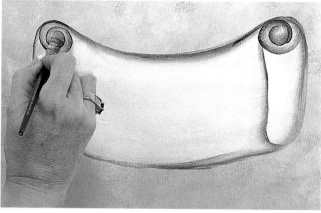

18 Switch to a no. 12 flat sideloaded into Raw Umber to stroke in the centers of the rolled edges. Follow the spiraling line of the rolled edge with the Raw Umber side of the brush.

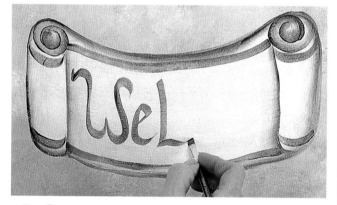

19 Use a no. 8 flat with Thicket and floating medium to add the borders and the lettering on the sign. When lettering, always use downward strokes. Make sure the lettering follows the slight curve of the sign.

20 Paint the thin post for the welcome sign using a no. 12 flat with Wicker White and Raw Umber. Switch to a no. 2 script liner and inky Raw Umber to add the little chain for the sign.

21 Paint the pole of the birdhouse using the chisel edge of a 1-inch (25mm) flat loaded with Raw Umber and floating medium.

22 Load a 1-inch (25mm) flat with Thicket, Sunflower and Wicker White, and add vines on the welcome sign pole, the birdhouse post and the tree trunk. Also fill in the blades of grass and the flower stems. Use your whole arm when stroking in the blades of grass and stems. Stroke upward from the base, slightly lifting the front of the brush at the end of the stroke for a nice pointed tip.

23 With the same brush and colors, paint in some large leaves where the wildflowers will go. Add floating medium to your brush and add a few shadow leaves in the background.

24 Use a 1-inch (25mm) flat double loaded with Yellow Light and Pure Orange to paint the orange cone-flowers. Lead with the Yellow Light side, pulling toward the flower center. Once in a while flip the brush so the Pure Orange side is leading; this gives the flower color variation. Add a little Engine Red to the Pure Orange side of the brush to create the red coneflowers.

25 Double load a small scruffy with Yellow Light and Thicket and pounce in the flower centers. Keep the Thicket side facing the petals. Come back in with Berry Wine and pounce this in on one side of the flower center and along the petal line for shading.

26 Use a 1-inch (25mm) flat with Thicket, Sunflower and Wicker White to add one-stroke leaves to the wisteria vine. Add curlicues with inky Thicket on a no. 2 script liner (the curlicues can be added before or after the wisteria). Load a large scruffy with Dioxazine Purple, Wicker White and Dark Plum and pounce in the wisteria blossoms, letting them trail off to a point. Don't overblend; keep them airy looking.

27 Add large leaves and one-stroke leaves to the birdhouse pole vine using Thicket, Sunflower and Wicker White on a 1-inch (25mm) flat. Use a no. 12 flat with Night Sky and Wicker White to paint the morning glory buds.

28 With the same brush and colors, paint the trumpet-shaped bottom of the flower, allowing the blue edge of the brush to paint the shape.

29 Still using the same brush and colors, paint the petals, keeping the Night Sky to the outside edge. Touch the chisel, make a little scallop by using a little pressure, then lift back up to the chisel. Repeat as you go around to complete the petal.

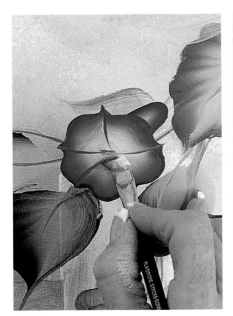

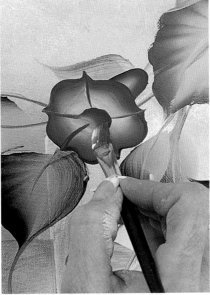

30 Use the chisel edge of your brush to paint in the ribs of the flower. Begin at the outside edge of the petal and pull in to the center, leading with the white.

31 The inside of the morning glory's trumpet is formed with a C-shaped stroke.

32 Use a no. 10 flat with Thicket and Yellow Light to lightly stroke in the stamens.

33 Double load Engine Red and Wicker White on a no. 12 flat and add phlox to the morning glory vine. Keep the Engine Red side of the brush to the outside and make simple five-petal blossoms, overlapping some of them to create a cluster. Dot in the centers with Yellow Light.

34 Load a large scruffy with Thicket, Sunflower and Wicker White and pounce moss along the bottom of the fence. Pounce random mounds rather than a straight line.

35 To paint the bluebird, use a no. 12 flat double loaded with Night Sky and Wicker White, picking up more paint as needed. The first stroke for the bird's head is a half circle, up and over.

36 The bird's back is one long stroke. Begin on the chisel edge of the brush, push, slide and lift back up to the chisel edge. Keep the blue side of the brush facing upward.

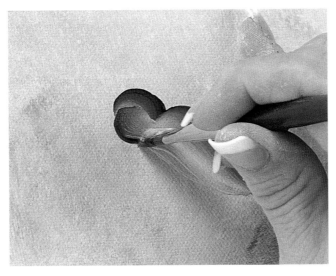

37 To paint the cheek, flip the brush so the blue is facing outward and paint a small C-stroke inside the round area of the head.

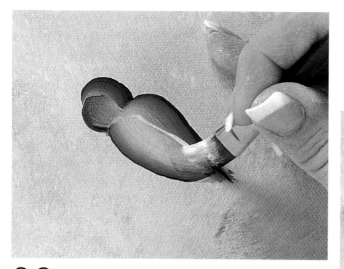

38 With the brush still facing in the same direction, stroke in the chest and belly.

39 Beginning right where the head and back meet, stroke in the back wing, keeping the blue side of the brush towards the top.

40 Pull feathers into the wing using a no. 12 flat with Night Sky and Wicker White. Lead with the white edge of the brush and stroke in to the white edge of the wing. Keep these feather strokes evenly spaced, and curve and shorten them a little more as they get closer to the body.

41 Stroke in the front wing and feathers in the same manner as the back wing. Be sure to stay on the chisel edge of your brush to keep the strokes feathery looking.

42 Add three tail feathers using the same strokes and colors you used for the wing feathers. Then using Yellow Light, add a few more feathers on the front wing and on the tail feathers as shown.

43 Finish the bluebird by adding the eye and the beak. With a no. 2 script liner, use Licorice for the eye and Yellow Ochre for the beak. Add a tiny highlight in the eye with Wicker White and little black dots on the top of the beak.

44 Finish the mural by pouncing in some moss on parts of the fence as shown.

breakaway wall mural

AS YOU HAVE PROBABLY NOTICED, breakaway walls are a very popular design element. They are a quick, easy and surprising decorative effect that you can add to your own home.

Paint an urn filled with topiaries or a ficus tree in your hall or entryway. Urns are perfect for those areas where you want to add some pizzazz but there's no room for you to hang pictures or set planters.

—— WHAT YOU'LL NEED ——

PAINT > Plaid FolkArt   (AP) = Plaid FolkArt Artists' Pigment

| Thicket | Wicker White | Raw Umber (AP) | Linen | Sunflower | Butter Pecan |

BRUSHES > 1-inch (25mm) flat, no. 8 flat, no. 2 script liner, large scruffy. **ADDITIONAL SUPPLIES >** floating medium, FolkArt One-Stroke Sponge Painters (or a regular foam sponge cut to shape), Plaid's urn stencil, Plaid's brick stencil, pencil, level, toothbrush. **PATTERN >** I encourage you to paint this mural freehand, but if you need a pattern, trace the finished painting at left and enlarge as needed. **SURFACE >** Interior wall painted with latex or acrylic paint in a satin or eggshell finish

1 Using a pencil, lightly trace the outside edge of the urn stencil on your wall for the basic shape of the urn (or trace the finished painting on page 96 and make a pattern). You may want to use a level to make sure the bottom of the stencil is properly aligned with your floor or baseboard.

2 Remove the stencil and basecoat the urn with Linen using the rounded-end One-Stroke Sponge Painter or a regular foam sponge cut to shape.

3 Reapply the stencil and use a 1-inch (25mm) flat, double loaded with Linen and Raw Umber, to dab along the dotted openings of the stencil.

4 Remove the stencil. The dots you see indicate all the raised surfaces of the urn.

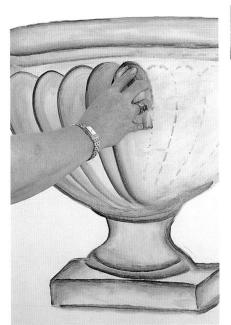

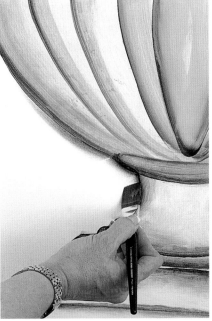

5 Load your sponge painter with Linen, dip the outside edge into Raw Umber and define the curves and edges of the urn, following the dots as shown.

6 Using the same colors on a 1-inch (25mm) flat, go back and further define the curves and edges. Also shade along the left side of the urn with Raw Umber and floating medium; keep the Raw Umber side against the urn and follow its contour.

7 Double load a 1-inch (25mm) flat with Linen and Raw Umber and, leading with the Linen, stroke in the stems of the topiary. Make them criss-cross over top of each other.

8 Load a large scruffy with Thicket, Sunflower and Wicker White (occasionally picking up Raw Umber and Butter Pecan) and pounce in moss around the top edge of the urn. Add some shadowing under the moss using a 1-inch (25mm) flat with Raw Umber and floating medium.

Load a sponge painter with Thicket, Sunflower and Wicker White and use a circular motion to sponge in foliage on the topiary. Go back in with a large scruffy and soften the circles on the topiary.

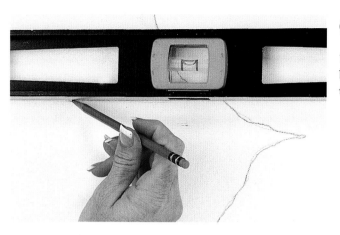

9 Draw the outside shape of the breakaway section onto your wall. Use a level and draw one line across the broken away section to designate a place to align the brick stencil.

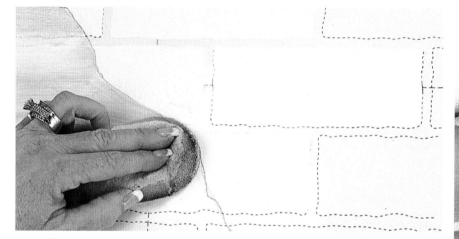

10 Line up the brick stencil with the drawn line. Use the sponge painter and alternately pick up Linen, Wicker White, Butter Pecan and Raw Umber to paint the bricks. Begin by laying the sponge painter at the edge of the breakaway line, then pull across each brick section. Move the stencil as needed until the entire breakaway section is filled in.

11 Before shadowing, be sure the bricks are thoroughly dry. You can use a hair dryer if needed. Load Raw Umber and floating medium on a 1-inch (25mm) flat to shadow the inside of one edge and the outside of the opposite edge of the breakaway section. Also extend a crack up from the breakaway section.

12 Use an old toothbrush with inky Raw Umber to splatter the bricks and give them a textured look.

13 Double load Raw Umber and floating medium on the chisel edge of a 1-inch (25mm) flat and add vines coming out from the corners of the breakaway area.

14 Paint a variety of leaves on the vine with a 1-inch (25mm) flat multiloaded with Thicket, Sunflower and Wicker White. Also add extra wispy vines using the chisel edge of the brush and leading with the light color. Use a no. 2 script liner and inky Thicket to add curlicues.

15 If you want to add vines growing up and around the topiary foliage, use a 1-inch (25mm) flat with Raw Umber and Wicker White. To add little one-stroke leaves to the vines on the light side of the foliage, use a no. 8 flat with Thicket and floating medium. On the dark side of the foliage, add a tiny bit of Sunflower to the leaves to make them lighter. Using inky Raw Umber, add some curlicues with your no. 2 script liner.

16 Here is the completed mural. Remember, use the elements you like and enjoy your design.

birdbath mural

KEEP A GARDEN BLOOMING all year 'round in your home, on a patio or even in a storefront window with this lattice trellis and birdbath. Add any flowers that you like or that match your decor.

The birdbath is a fun and interesting element in this garden scene. You could even add a few little garden animals among the flowers if you like.

Finish the garden scene with greenery, ferns and lots of flowers.

—— WHAT YOU'LL NEED ——

PAINT > Plaid FolkArt   (AP) = Plaid FolkArt Artists' Pigment

School Bus Yellow | Wicker White | Thicket | Berry Wine | Sunflower | Dioxazine Purple (AP)

Yellow Light (AP) | French Blue | Cobalt (AP) | Dove Gray | Heather | Grass Green

Licorice | Yellow Ochre (AP) | Midnight

BRUSHES > ¾-inch (19mm) flat, 1-inch (25mm) flat, 1-½ inch (38 mm) flat, no. 12 flat, no. 2 script liner, scruffy. **ADDITIONAL SUPPLIES >** FolkArt One-Stroke Sponge Painters (or a regular foam sponge cut to shape), floating medium. **SURFACE >** Interior wall painted with latex or acrylic paint in a satin or eggshell finish.

This pattern may be hand-traced or photocopied for personal use only. Enlarge as needed for your wall space.

1 Basecoat the sky using the One-Stroke Sponge Painter (or a regular foam sponge cut to shape) loaded with Wicker White, French Blue and just a tiny bit of Sunflower. Use floating medium as needed for smooth strokes. Alternate between these colors and use long side-to-side strokes to fill in the sky area.

To fill in the grass area, load the sponge painter with Thicket, Sunflower and Wicker White and use the same long, side-to-side strokes. Use floating medium to smooth out the strokes if needed. Let dry.

2 Trace the trellis and birdbath patterns onto the background. Load Wicker White on a sponge painter and, with a circular motion, add clouds.

3 Basecoat the birdbath with Wicker White using a sponge painter. Clean up the edges with a 1-1/2 inch (38mm) flat. Using the same brush with Wicker White, basecoat the trellis. When it's dry, you can trace on the details if needed.

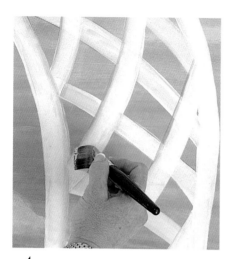

5 Use a 1-inch (25mm) flat with the same colors to shade the birdbath as shown.

4 Use a 1-¹/₂ inch (38mm) flat with floating medium, Wicker White and Dove Gray to shade the trellis. Decide which side you want to shade and keep the shading consistent throughout the trellis.

6 Add vines and leaves to the trellis with a 1-inch (25mm) flat loaded with Thicket, Wicker White and Sunflower. (See pages 28-34 for complete step-by-step instructions.)

Add cabbage roses to the vine with Berry Wine and Wicker White on a 1-inch (25mm) flat. (See pages 45-46 for step-by-step cabbage rose instructions).

7 This is how your trellis-and-birdbath mural looks so far.

8 Double load Cobalt and Wicker White on a 1-inch (25mm) flat to stroke water into the birdbath. Add highlights using the chisel edge of the brush and leading with the white. The strokes should follow the curve of the birdbath.

9 Using Midnight, Wicker White and Berry Wine and a no. 12 flat, stroke in the splashing bluebird. (See pages 93-95 for step-by-step instructions on painting a bluebird.) Paint the bird's beak with a no. 2 script liner and Yellow Ochre. Load the same brush with inky Licorice and add eyes and beak details. Dip the tip of the brush into Wicker White to add eye highlights.

To make the water look like the bird is playing in it, dab in some Wicker White, then immediately dab in a little Cobalt. Also add some watery ripples around the bird with the same colors.

10 Paint the yellow-breasted birds using Licorice, School Bus Yellow and Wicker White. Add their little beaks and eyes. There are two yellow birds on the birdbath and one on top of the trellis.

11 Paint the hummingbirds. For their backs and wings, use Thicket and Wicker White. For the belly and face, use Berry Wine and Wicker White. Use a no. 2 script liner with inky Thicket to add the eyes and beaks.

12 Feel free to add more birds if you like. I added another bluebird flying above the birdbath, and another yellow-breasted bird near the top of the trellis.

13 Pick up Thicket on your sponge painter and with a back-and-forth stroke, shade around the base of the birdbath forward into the foreground. Pick up a tiny bit of Dove Gray once in a while to add some color variation.

Use a 1-inch (25mm) flat alternating between Thicket, Grass Green and Wicker White to stroke in the grass blades on the left side of the trellis. The grass in the background should be a lighter green and the grass in the foreground a deeper, more intense green.

14 On the right side of the trellis, use the same brush with Thicket, Wicker White and lots of floating medium to stroke in the shadow ferns in the background.

15 Using the same brush with Thicket and Wicker White, add the ferns, grass and the large leaves. Load Dioxazine Purple and Heather on a no. 12 flat to add the violets. Dab in little light touches of the color (almost like shadow flowers) in the background. With the tip of a no. 2 script liner, dip into Sunflower and dab in the violet centers. Add the butterflies with Wicker White and School Bus Yellow (see page 42 for butterfly instructions).

Use a 1-inch (25mm) flat with Wicker White and Thicket to add one-stroke leaves to the trellis. With a no. 2 script liner and inky Thicket, add curlicues.

16 On the left side of the trellis base, paint in the lupines using a no. 12 flat with Wicker White and Yellow Light. Stroke in a little teardrop shape for each petal, keeping the white to the outside.

17 Use the chisel edge of a 1-inch (25mm) flat loaded with Dioxazine Purple and Heather to paint in the lavender blossoms.

18 Add the large leaves around the Queen Anne's Lace using a 1-inch (25mm) flat with Thicket, Wicker White and Sunflower. Paint the stems of the Queen Anne's Lace with Grass Green and Thicket. Then use a large scruffy to pounce in Wicker White to form the lacy flower-heads.

19 Finish your mural with a few blades of grass around the base of the birdbath, using Thicket, Grass Green and Wicker White.

metallic wall treatment

SCENIC MURALS are not the only way to dress up your walls. Here is a sophisticated wall treatment that incorporates three different but harmonious elements: a border, a striped wallpaper effect, and a fern design. The colors can be changed to suit your decor; the ferns can be replaced with another design of your choice, and of course the stripes can be made whatever width or pattern you like. Have fun and experiment!

To change the color, find a FolkArt Metallic color that you like. Then pick a background color that is similar, either darker or lighter, but not exactly the same color. If you want to keep your wall the color you have, compare a swatch of that color to the FolkArt Metallic colors and find one that is close, but not exactly the same. An example would be Metallic Champagne with a Linen background. You may prefer more or less contrast between colors—it's your choice.

You also may prefer a different border design. On a Linen and Champagne Metallic wall, try the fern and rose border shown on page 43 painted with Butter Pecan, Linen and Wicker White. The variations are limitless.

─── WHAT YOU'LL NEED ───

PAINT > Plaid FolkArt   M = Plaid FolkArt Metallics

Metallic Peridot (M)	Thicket	Wicker White

BRUSHES > 1-inch (25mm) flat. **ADDITIONAL SUPPLIES >** floating medium, water-based exterior varnish, small sponge paint roller, 1-inch (25mm) painter's tape, level and pencil. **PATTERN >** If you need a pattern for the ferns, trace the finished painting on the facing page and enlarge as needed. **SURFACE >** Interior wall painted with a latex or acrylic paint in a satin or eggshell finish.

1 Basecoat your walls with a latex or acrylic interior paint in a satin or eggshell finish, in a color of your choosing. Allow the paint to dry completely according to the manufacturer's instructions.

Use a level or yardstick (meterstick) to mark off a horizontal line around the wall where you want the bottom of the metallic fern border to be. Using 1-inch (25mm) painter's tape, tape above the horizontal marks. Now mark off a vertical line with your level.

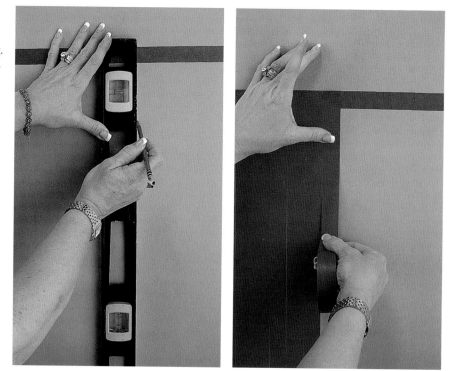

2 Use the vertical mark as a guide for applying painter's tape vertically side-by-side along the wall as shown.

3 Decide how wide you want your stripes to be and what the repeating pattern will be, then pull off the tape where you want to paint with the Metallic color.

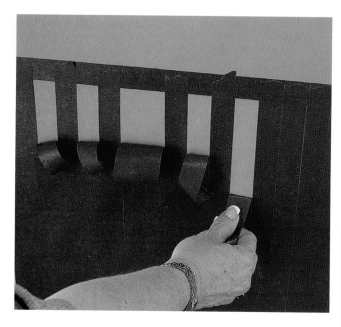

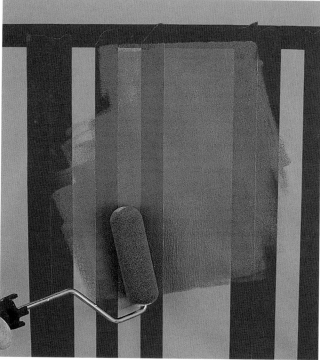

4 Use a small sponge roller to roll on the paint that you want to use for the stripes. This is Metallic Peridot.

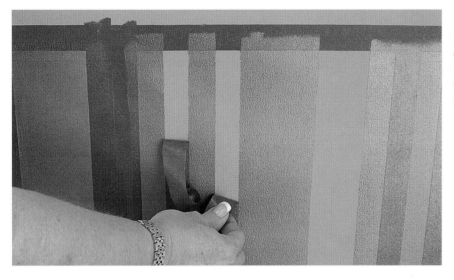

5 Pull off the tape right after the paint is applied. It's best to pull the tape off while the paint is still wet. If you wait until the paint completely dries, some of the paint may pull off with the tape. You may want to paint this in sections.

6 Allow the stripes to dry completely. This may take up to twenty-four hours. Once dry, apply a strip of painter's tape right across the top of the stripes that you have already painted as shown.

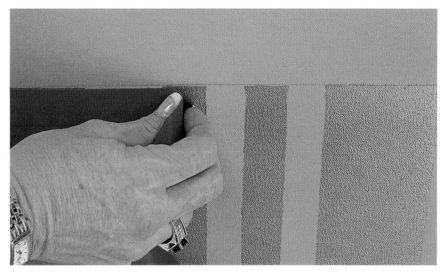

7 Measure 9 inches (23cm) up from the top edge of the strip of tape you just applied and make a mark on the wall. Use your level and pencil to mark a horizontal line around the room for the top of the border. Apply painter's tape above this line (be sure it is above and not below the penciled line). Use a sponge roller to apply the border color (this is Metallic Peridot). Pull off the tape and let the paint dry completely.

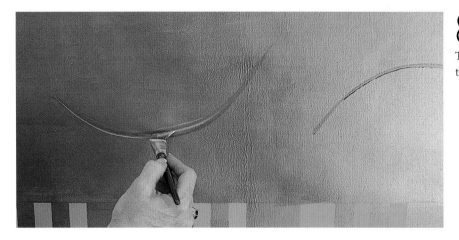

8 When the border color is dry, double load a 1-inch (25mm) flat with Thicket and Wicker White and paint in the stems of the fern fronds.

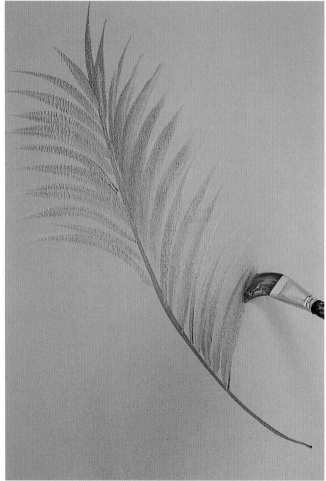

9 Using the same colors and brush, paint the fern leaflets coming off of the stems (see page 44 for hints on painting ferns). The unique look of this wall treatment is achieved by using a flat paint when painting on top of metallic paint, and using a metallic paint when painting on top of a satin or eggshell paint. It's the contrast between the flat or satin paint and the metallic paint that gives this treatment a sophisticated, contemporary look.

10 On the wall area above the border, use the same brush with a lot of Metallic Peridot, a little bit of Wicker White and a little bit of Thicket to paint a variety of fern fronds (see picture at right for placement ideas).

11 Paint the fern fronds at different angles as you evenly space them out on the wall. Paint some from the front, some from the back, and some arching downward.

floral wall treatment

THIS HANDPAINTED WALL TREATMENT is an easy way to dramatically change a room. I love the fresh combination of the soft pink with the bright flowers. Shadowing the flowers and leaves really gives depth and dimension to the design.

Make this design your own. You can change the color combinations to match your home, or you can add or eliminate flowers and leaves as you desire.

—— WHAT YOU'LL NEED ——

PAINT > Plaid FolkArt   (AP) = Plaid FolkArt Artists' Pigment

| Taffy | Wicker White | Buttercrunch | Grass Green | Thicket | Engine Red |

| School Bus Yellow | Yellow Light (AP) | Licorice |

BRUSHES > 1-inch (25mm) flat, no. 2 script liner, large scruffy. **ADDITIONAL SUPPLIES** > FolkArt One-Stroke Sponge Painters (or a regular foam sponge cut to shape), 1-inch (25mm) and 1-½ inch (38mm) wide painter's tape, level, pencil, floating medium. **PATTERN** > I encourage you to paint this design freehand, but if you need a pattern, trace the finished wall treatment on the facing page and enlarge as needed. **SURFACE** > Interior wall painted with latex or acrylic paint in a satin or eggshell finish.

1 Basecoat the wall with a latex or acrylic paint in a satin or eggshell finish in a color of your choice. I used Taffy on this wall. Allow the paint to dry completely before applying painter's tape. Measure up from the floor and mark where you want the bottom of the border to be. Using a level, mark around the room, then apply painter's tape below the marks. Decide how wide you want your border to be and measure up from the tape. Use a level and mark the top of the border around the room. Tape off the top of the border above the marks.

2 Load a large sponge with Taffy and lots of Wicker White and pounce in the border background.

3 Once the paint has thoroughly dried, apply two or more strips of tape right inside the previous strips. Remove the middle strip of tape. This is where you will be painting the stripes.

4 Use your 1-inch (25 mm) flat with Buttercrunch to paint the stripes; you will need two coats. Remove the tape.

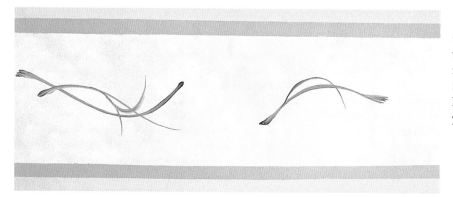

5 After the border background paint is dry, load a 1-inch (25mm) brush with Grass Green, Thicket and floating medium and stroke in the flower stems. Start up on the chisel edge, then add a little more pressure on your brush where you want the stems to be thicker.

6 Now load a 1-inch (25mm) flat with Engine Red, School Bus Yellow and Wicker White and paint the flower petals. Keep the lighter color to the outside edge. Begin on the chisel edge on one side of the stem, then push, wiggle out and slide back in. Vary the length of the petals as shown.

7 Continue to add these in-and-out petals until you get to the other side of the stem, then lift back up to the chisel edge. As you lift, flip the brush so the light color is on the other side; this will make the petal look as if it has turned.

8 Load School Bus Yellow, Thicket and a touch of Yellow Light on a large scruffy and pounce in the flower center. Keep the Thicket facing toward the top of the flower.

9 Once the flower center has dried, add the overlapping petal. Use the same brush, colors and stroke described in steps 6 and 7 above.

10 Load a 1-inch (25mm) flat with Grass Green, Thicket and floating medium, and use the chisel edge of the brush to grab wet paint at the base of the flower and pull out to connect to the stem.

11 Paint the leaves using a 1-inch (25mm) flat loaded with Thicket and Grass Green. See pages 13-19 for step-by-step leaf painting instructions.

12 Load a no. 2 script liner with an inky mixture of Thicket and Yellow Light. Pull stamen lines from the flower center. Then using the same mixture and brush, dab pollen onto the tips.

13 Load a 1-inch (25mm) flat with floating medium, then drag an edge of the bristles along a puddle of Thicket. Add shadows by floating the color alongside the leaves and stem that you just painted.

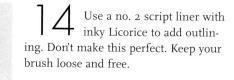

14 Use a no. 2 script liner with inky Licorice to add outlining. Don't make this perfect. Keep your brush loose and free.

15 Load a 1-inch (25mm) flat with Thicket, Grass Green and floating medium and paint the shadow leaves on the bottom section of the wall. See the photo below for placement ideas.

16 Scatter flowers and leaves, such as the ones above, throughout the top section of the wall wherever you like. Use the same instructions and colors you used for the flowers and leaves inside the border (see pages 119-120).

17 Here is the completed wall treatment—a lovely and interesting design for almost any room in your home. Remember, you can choose any element in any of these designs, change the colors, combine them as you like, and make them your own.

starting your own muraling business

I believe it's always best to begin painting on walls for fun and to enhance your own home decor. However, there may come a time when you feel ready to take the next step and paint murals for profit. Over the years I have learned quite a bit from having my own design and mural painting business. I'm happy to have this opportunity to share with you what has worked best for me. I hope to equip you with some business basics so that you are one step closer to starting your own business. You may not be ready yet, but if and when you are, just pick up this book and you will be on your way.

GETTING STARTED

In the beginning, when you are painting murals, borders and wall treatments for family and friends for free, keep track of your time. This will help when you do begin painting for profit as you will have a gauge by which to measure.

It is important to treat these first "not-for-profit" customers just as if they were paying customers. Talk with them about their wishes and ideas for the design. You may need to go outside of your comfort zone in order to please them by painting what they request and where they request it (if possible). This will be a great learning experience for you; it will improve your communication skills and will also help you to understand a customer's wishes.

PAINTING FOR FREE

No, I'm not crazy—painting for free works! Let me explain. Consider painting a mural in a beauty shop, a doctor's or dentist's office, daycare center, or any office with a busy waiting room. Select an area that will be seen by everyone, or nearly everyone, who enters that business. Once you have decided where you want to paint, approach the office manager, owner or other responsible person to discuss your proposition. Explain that in return for painting the mural, you would like to leave your business card so that potential clients can contact you directly. Be sure to conduct yourself in a professional manner when you meet with the owner and while you are painting.

It is important to return to these locations on a regular basis to touch up or even to update the painting. This is an unexpected service that shows you care.

PAINT EVERYWHERE

When considering where to paint for free or even where to look for paid work, be creative. I have painted on the interior of a mobile mammogram unit, in recreational vehicles, in school cafeterias and hallways, local boys' and girls' clubs, community centers, and many more.

Painting in a variety of places exposes your work to people from all walks of life. Do the unexpected and don't limit yourself. You will be amazed at the response you'll receive!

MODEL HOME OPPORTUNITIES

All sorts of people tour the model home shows, which makes these shows a wonderful opportunity for exposure to your work. Whether you paint murals in model homes for free or not is up to you; however, you may find they can be very conducive to your success. Once again it is imperative that you provide a means by which potential clients can contact you, such as business cards or flyers. Some of my most successful painting jobs have come from this opportunity. One time a builder actually featured my painting in his listing as an added incentive for potential buyers.

ADVERTISING

I am not an expert on advertising but I am willing to share with you what has worked for me. Without a doubt, word of mouth has been the very best method of advertising for my business. Satisfied customers sell my work to potential customers much better than I ever could. Many times I find myself returning to the same neighborhood again and again. Returning to the same area within the same group of friends or neighbors is the best way to track the success of word-of-mouth advertising. Don't ever underestimate this form of getting the word out about your business.

Flyers and locally distributed publications such as small newspapers or weekly advertising throws are another possible means of getting your name out to the public. I find it necessary to include some kind of cut-out coupon when using this kind of advertising so I can keep track of the return for the dollar spent.

PRICING

One of the questions I am most frequently asked by people starting out on their own is how to know what to charge a client. There is no set method or formula for figuring this out that I am aware of, but the method that I use works in most instances and allows me to price myself according to my abilities and personal speed. This method should give you the basics to figure out what you might charge for your services.

The standard in the muraling business is to quote your prices on a per job basis. To determine this rate, paint a test project. First, pick a room in your home or a friend's home, choose a basic design and gather up the supplies and tools you will need for the job. Next, write down a few notes regarding the plan, especially how you envision the finished wall. Let's say that you have a 10-foot (3m) x 12-foot (3.6m) bedroom and you are painting a vine with trailing flowers around the room. You are painting at an 8-foot (2.4m) height. This is a standard commission you may find yourself painting quite often.

Once your room size and design are determined, you're ready to paint! Begin timing yourself from the time you enter the room until you finish painting and cleaning up. Keep a careful and accurate account of your time. This is necessary for you to calculate a fair and honest rate for your customers and for yourself. Let's say that this test project takes you 4 hours to paint.

Next you will need to decide upon an hourly rate. Do a little research where you live and find out what mural painters in your area charge, then set your rates accordingly. The rates in most areas fall between $50 and $100 (U.S.) per hour. This may sound high, but your rate must take into account all pricing factors such as travel time, difficulty of the job and special tools needed (see Pricing Factors, below). You will be constantly adjusting your rate depending on these factors, charging a higher rate for a more difficult job.

The hourly rate determination is for your information only—it is not discussed with the customer. The hourly rate is simply a tool you will use for calculating the estimate for each job. The price you will quote the customer is the final, all-inclusive total for their job.

Using our test project as an example, you may choose an hourly rate of $50 because the job is very straightforward. Your price to paint the room would be $50 x 4 hours, or $200. If a similar job were at a site some distance from your house, you might increase your hourly rate to, say, $60 to cover your travel expenses. So your price to paint a room at that more distant site would be $60 x 4 hours, or $240. When the customer inquires as to cost, simply give the customer an estimated price of around $240 to $300. Don't state a definite price until the job is completely finished. You should always allow room to adjust the price for unforeseen circumstances.

Now, of course, this example serves only as a basic place for you to start. You will need to continually keep track of the time you spend on each job and continue to evaluate, update and assess yourself and your rate. This is how I started and have found the method 99% accurate in most instances. Some jobs will be easier while others will be more difficult, but the more jobs you do, the easier it will be to evaluate the true cost of each job.

PRICING FACTORS

When determining your per-job price, you'll need to consider these additional factors.

• Ceiling height. The higher the ceiling, the costlier the job. If you are painting borders or designs above 8 feet (2.4m), be sure to allow for additional time and possible assistance, as the repetition of going up and down ladders or scaffolding can be time consuming.

• Assistance. If the job is too large to complete by yourself, be sure to factor in the cost of an assistant.

• Travel expenses. If you will be traveling out of your immediate area, allow extra for the travel time and gas.

• Special tools. Will the job require special faux finishing tools, cloths, sponges that go beyond what you figure are your basic tools?

• Additional supplies. If a job is very large, be sure to add in the cost of brushes, paper towels and paints that go beyond your basic supplies.

COMMUNICATING WITH THE CLIENT

Before you start a job, spend some time talking to your client. Following are some questions you need to ask and some important things you will want to discuss with them, such as:

• Ask how they heard about your work. You will need to have this information to keep track of where your advertising dollars are most effective.

• Ask for explicit directions to the site. This is very important and can be a real time saver.

• Ask the height of the ceiling so you know which ladders and scaffolding to bring.

• Discuss what kinds of designs they like. Prepare an "idea book" of designs for discussion if requested.

• Ask what their favorite colors are. Some colors are very hard to mix on site, so you will want to purchase these colors ahead of time.

Be sure that the customer has done his homework too. Ask him to provide photos of the golf course with that special hole that he wants painted. Pictures of what customers want really help to clarify their desires!

ARRIVE PREPARED

Be sure you have all the supplies you need for each specific job. You may find that keeping a list helps. Check your list before you leave home to make sure you have everything. Remember any special tools, like stencils or faux finishing tools, you'll need for the job. Will you need an overhead projector if the client supplies you with a photograph? Or if the client doesn't have a photo, do you have your idea book with you as inspiration?

Having a list to refer to keeps you more organized right from the start. As you gain experience, it will become easier to prepare for each job.

PREVENTING PROBLEMS

I make the customer aware right up front that I do have a minimum charge for each job and that I am unable to give free estimates. This of course is a personal choice, but you are in business and you should be fair to yourself; your time is valuable.

If you don't require a minimum charge for every job, you will find yourself spending a lot of time doing very small jobs that don't pay for your travel or time.

I also charge for estimates. If you don't charge for estimates, you will need to recoup your cost of travel and time spent estimating in other ways. The cost will need to be calculated into your expenses, therefore costing each customer more whether they receive an estimate or not.

One way I alleviate the problem of potential customers requesting free estimates is this: I simply say, "Due to my schedule it is very difficult for me to provide free estimation time; what I usually like to do is come ready to paint. If we are able to agree upon a design and price, I will paint; if not, then I will estimate the cost and reschedule the painting for another time." If I actually have to give an estimate and not paint, I will calculate the cost of the estimate into the job. Usually I am able to negotiate an agreement while I'm there.

Another problem I have encountered is the customer who agrees to a price but is unable to afford it all at once. I have a simple solution. I explain to them that I can paint the design in stages and I will begin today and paint only as much as they can afford. As soon as they are able to afford more, they can call and schedule my return. Hint: By using the murals in this book you could paint a separate element each visit so your work does not look incomplete. Be sure to factor in the return time and associated travel expenses when working this way.

FINAL THOUGHTS

With each job you will gain experience and learn what works best for you. I hope sharing what I have learned over the years has inspired you to think about starting your own muraling business some day.

I would like to share one of my painting experiences with you. A potential customer contacted me concerning a somewhat delicate request in reference to a painting job. The customer and her decorator had agreed on a plan to include a wall painting which would be incorporated into the actual window treatments. The plan was to have a spray of flowers trailing off the drapery material in a few areas. This didn't seem difficult, and I really did not think I'd have any problem meeting their request. I arrived at the job and was ready to go when the curve ball was thrown. The color of the ribbon holding the flower bunches together was the most unusual shade of glittery green I had ever seen, and it was to be painted throughout the design.

After a few minutes of color mixing and a little prayer, I came up with a possible match. The customer approved the color and all

seemed well until I ran into Murphy's law, the law that says, "If something can go wrong, it will." The shade I had mixed looked just right on my palette, but when I applied the color to the white wall, it looked very different.

I re-mixed the color numerous times, each time testing it on the wall and quickly wiping it off before it dried. This went on for close to thirty minutes. Then again I asked the customer for approval while giving an apologetic explanation for my previous premature color approval. This time she seemed a little less confident in my ability and took a much longer time to approve my concoction. You can only imagine how nervous I was by then.

There is a good ending to this story, however: the paint color turned out beautifully (that is, if you like a sort of "swampy" green color with sparkles) and the customer was delighted. The job turned out well, and in the process I learned a valuable lesson in humility. Every wall painting job I have ever done has offered me this lesson, for just as soon as I feel comfortable, I realize I still have lots to learn.

Even with all the walls I have painted and all the homes and businesses I have painted in, each experience has been unique. It seems as though no matter what the design or the circumstance, each job has enlightened me a little more. My talents are on loan, and I know that as I share them I continue to be blessed more than I could have ever imagined.

May you experience the same blessing whether you paint one room or one hundred rooms. May your life and those around you be enriched and beautified, and may you leave a little piece of your heart on each and every wall you paint.

resources

Dewberry Designs
124 Robin Rd., Suite 1700
Altamonte Springs, FL 32701
Phone (407) 339-0239
FAX (407) 339-5513
E-mail: dewberry@magicnet.com
www.onestroke.com

Plaid Enterprises
3225 Westech Drive
Norcross, GA 30092
Phone (678) 291-8100
FAX (678) 291-8156
www.plaidonline.com

Retailers in Canada

Crafts Canada
2745 Twenty-ninth St. NE
Calgary, Alberta T1Y 7B5

Folk Art Enterprises
P.O. Box 1088
Ridgetown, Ontario N0P 2C0
(888) 214-0062

MacPherson Craft Wholesale
83 Queen St. E.
P.O. Box 1870
St. Mary's, Ontario N4X 1C2
(519) 284-1741

Maureen McNaughton Enterprises
RR #2
Belwood, Ontario N0B 1J0
(519) 843-5648

Mercury Art & Craft Supershop
332 Wellington St.
London, Ontario N6C 4P7
(519) 434-1636

Town & Country Folk Art Supplies
93 Green Lane
Thornhill, Ontario L3T 6K6
(905) 882-0199

Retailers in the United Kingdom

Art Express
Index House
70 Burley Road
Leeds LS3 1JX
Tel: 0800 731 4185
www.artexpress.co.uk

Crafts World
No 8 North Street
Guildford
Surrey GU1 4AF
Tel: 07000 757070
Chroma Colour Products
Unit 5 Pilton Estate

Pitlake
Croydon CR0 3RA
Tel: 020 8688 1991
www.chromacolour.com

Green & Stone
259 King's Road
London SW3 5EL
Tel: 020 7352 0837
greenandstone@enterprise.net

Hobbycrafts
River Court
Southern Sector
Bournemouth International Airport
Christchurch
Dorset BH23 6SE
Tel: 0800 272387

Homecrafts Direct
P.O. Box 38
Leicester LE1 9BU
Tel: 0116 251 3139

index

Explore the world of decorative painting with North Light Books!

Let Michelle Temares show you how to develop, draw, transfer and paint your own original designs for everything from furniture and decorative accessories to walls and interior décor. "Good" and "bad" examples illustrate each important lesson, while three step-by-step decorative painting projects help you make the leap from initial idea to completed composition!

ISBN 1-58180-263-3, paperback, 128 pages, #32128-K

Learn how to enhance your paintings with the classic elegance of decorative gold, silver and variegated accents. Rebecca Baer illustrates detailed gilding techniques with step-by-step photos and invaluable problem-solving advice. Perfect for your home or gift giving, there are 13 exciting projects in all, each one enhanced with lustrous leafing effects.

ISBN 1-58180-261-7, paperback, 144 pages, #32126-K

Add drama to any room in your home with one of these 11 delightful mini-murals! They're perfect for when you don't have the time or the experience to tackle a whole wall. You'll learn which colors and brushes to use, plus tips and mini-demos for getting the realistic effects you love. Includes detailed templates, photos and step-by-step instructions.

ISBN 1-58180-145-9, paperback, 144 pages, #31891-K

Add beauty and elegance to every room in your home! Diane Treirweiler shows you how with step-by-step instructions for giving old furniture a facelift and new furniture a personal touch. Twelve lovely projects, complete with helpful color charts and traceable patterns, teach you how to paint everything from berries to butterflies on chests, chairs, tables and more.

ISBN 1-58180-234-X, paperback, 128 pages, #32009-K

These books and other fine North Light titles are available from your local art & craft retailer, bookstore, online supplier or by calling 1-800-448-0915.